THE
WISDOM
of
GOD

THE
WISDOM
of GOD

LETTING HIS **TRUTH** AND **GOODNESS**
DIRECT YOUR STEPS

A.W. TOZER

JAMES L. SNYDER, COMPILER AND EDITOR

BETHANYHOUSE
a division of Baker Publishing Group
Minneapolis, Minnesota

© 2017 by James L. Snyder

Published by Bethany House Publishers
11400 Hampshire Avenue South
Bloomington, Minnesota 55438
www.bethanyhouse.com

Bethany House Publishers is a division of
Baker Publishing Group, Grand Rapids, Michigan

Printed in the United States of America

ISBN 978-0-7642-1808-8

Library of Congress Control Number: 2017936458

Scripture quotations are from the King James Version of the Bible.

Cover design by Rob Williams, InsideOutCreativeArts

James L. Snyder is represented by The Steve Laube Agency.

Contents

Introduction

There are known knowns—things we know we know," Donald Rumsfeld once famously said. And there are known unknowns—things we do not know. "But there are also unknown unknowns," the former U.S. Secretary of Defense added, "the ones we don't know we don't know."

Dr. Tozer would have said Amen to that most enthusiastically. As soon as a person admits he does not know everything, he is in a position to learn something.

What many people do not understand is that the unknown unknowns *can* and *do* sabotage lives. It is the arrogance of a fool who believes he knows everything and therefore qualifies him for making all the decisions in his life and that of others around him. This is especially true of the spiritual life.

Dr. Tozer presents in this book a question that needs serious pondering: "Why is it that man, with drastically limited wisdom, insists on making all the decisions in his life while a good portion of the time he is wrong?"

Tozer exhorts us to "go to God first." God's wisdom is the only absolute and unlimited wisdom. Tapping into His divine, eternal wisdom will change your life. How often do we make decisions based on human wisdom we have at the time only later to find out something that counters our decision?

We need to seek an *afflatus*, literally a breath, an inspiration of divine wisdom to invade our lives, Tozer says. Everything holy and good in this world has flowed from this wisdom. It is the work of the Holy Spirit in the life of the believer, making God's wisdom a reality in their life.

There is no question that human wisdom has accomplished much good in this world, but man's knowledge and wisdom can only go so far. It is limited. There is a ceiling that cannot be penetrated. A major concern of Tozer was for Christian leaders who tried to use human wisdom for what only can be accomplished through God's wisdom. Human talent, scholarship, experience, and entertainment run the church today. All these things are a substitute for God's wisdom, which cannot be earned. Rather, it is a gift of God that comes upon the believer as he yields himself to Jesus Christ.

To know Christ is to know God's wisdom. The more we understand this, the more we will be able to see the hand of God in our life moving us in the direction He wants us to go.

The amazing thing to me is that all the sermons that make up this book were preached in the early 1960s, but the message is relevant to Christianity today. What was true then is true today, if not more so.

This book outlines the progress of man's knowledge of divine wisdom, which has its roots in Hebrew doctrine. An interesting aspect is Dr. Tozer's use of two apocryphal books: *Wisdom of Solomon* and *Ecclesiasticus.* Although not inspired as are the sixty-six books of the Bible, they present the Hebrew doctrine of wisdom.

Tozer emphasizes the Pilgrim Way of our lives as a perilous way. Everything in this world is contradictory to the man or woman who is walking with God. In order to live the victorious Christian life, we must live in the power of God's wisdom. *Holy Spirit*

Rev. James L. Snyder, DLit

1

The Hebrew Doctrine of Wisdom

10·6·21

O God, Thou who art Eternal Wisdom, speak into my heart today that wisdom that will glorify Thee. I joyfully turn away from my human reasoning and trust Thy wisdom to guide me and direct me throughout my day.

Let me not succumb to the limitations of my own reasoning and knowledge but leap beyond that and step into the reality of Thy holy presence. Amen.

For a long time I have been thinking about the subject of this book, wisdom. A better writer than I should write this book, but in the meantime, I will do my best to unburden my heart. I hope my work will inspire someone to take it a step further.

The wisdom that enthralls me is not human wisdom, but rather eternal wisdom as it relates to Jesus Christ our Lord. I have studied human wisdom and secular psychology and know their weaknesses, or rather their conspicuous limitations.

In every culture, wisdom is shared specific to the people of that culture. Along with that are the limitations associated with the wisdom of a given culture. The wisdom of the human mind and imagination in any culture is limited.

However, when it comes to the doctrine of what I call *eternal wisdom*, it refers to the wisdom revealed through the Hebrew people, and that is the focus of this book: the Hebrew doctrine of wisdom. The Scriptures are full of this teaching in both the Old and the New Testaments. You cannot read the Psalms or Proverbs or Ecclesiastes without encountering the eternal wisdom of God. The Hebrews defined it supremely well from the very beginning, and that is what I want to examine in this book.

The Hebrew Understanding

The Hebrews believed there was an ancient, uncreated afflatus, or divine breath. It was variously thought of as apart from God, as being God himself, as being brought into being by God, or the gods, and other times it was thought of as bringing all things into being. The Old Testament is filled with this doctrine, and I want to look at it from the Hebrew understanding, but particularly as it is fulfilled in Jesus Christ.

This is not only an Old Testament doctrine. It comes very close to what John writes, "In the beginning was the Word, and the Word was with God, and the Word was God" (John 1:1). John in his writings is reflecting this Hebrew doctrine of eternal wisdom.

I want to include in this chapter what the Hebrews thought about this doctrine of eternal wisdom years before the book of Ecclesiastes was written. This would take us back approximately one thousand years before Christ. The *Wisdom of Solomon*, one of fifteen books of the Apocrypha, a collection probably not well-known in most evangelical circles, has an important application to what the Hebrews believed about wisdom.

> For wisdom, which is the worker of all things, taught me: for in her is an understanding spirit: holy, one only, manifold, subtle, lively, clear, undefiled, plain, not subject to hurt, loving the thing that is good, quick, which cannot be letted, ready to do good, kind to man, steadfast, sure, free from care, having all power, overseeing all things, and going through all understanding, pure, and most subtle spirits. For wisdom is more moving than any motion: she passeth and goeth through all things by reason of her pureness. For she is the breath of the power of God, and a pure influence flowing from the glory of the Almighty: therefore, can no defiled thing fall into her. For she is the brightness of the everlasting light, the unspotted mirror of the power of God, and the image of his goodness. And being but one, she can do all things; and remaining in herself, she maketh all things new; and in all ages entering into holy souls, she maketh them friends of God, and prophets. For God loveth none but him that dwelleth with wisdom. For she is more beautiful than the sun, and above all the order of stars: being compared with the light, she is found before

it. For after this cometh night, but vice shall not prevail against wisdom.

Wisdom of Solomon 7:22–30

I do not include this passage because I think it is inspired by God in the sense that Proverbs and Ecclesiastes are inspired. Rather, I include it as I might quote Charles Spurgeon, St. Augustine, or anyone who, though not Bible writers in the same sense, nevertheless, were students of the Bible, and therefore we can trust them as teachers of the Bible. Only the sixty-six books of the Bible are divinely inspired by God. The *Wisdom of Solomon* is not one of them, but rather is an important insight into the Hebrew doctrine of wisdom. It is important because it reveals the belief the ancients had about this subject.

Application of Hebrew Doctrine

I suggest you carefully read the *Wisdom of Solomon* passage again and notice how the language is similar to passages found in the Old and New Testaments, particularly in verses 25 and 26:

For she is the breath of the power of God, and a pure influence flowing from the glory of the Almighty: therefore, can no defiled thing fall into her. For she is the brightness of the everlasting light, the unspotted mirror of the power of God, and the image of his goodness.

The Scriptures teach and church fathers believed that the spirit described in the above passage is Christ, the wisdom of the Old Testament. *Sophia* was and is the Greek word used

14

in the Greek translation of the Old Testament as well as in Jesus' day for "wisdom." The church fathers echoed this.

Carried into the New Testament, it is seen, for example, when John wrote, "In the beginning was the Word." John was not identifying Christianity with the Greek thought of his day. Rather, he was using a Greek word to explain what God had to say. The word *logos* is the Greek word for "word" or "reason." Many theological liberals claim John wrote his gospel under the influence of Plato. Early Christianity, they argue, was strongly influenced by the Greek doctrine of the logos, the thought and expression of God, for one word will not define it. Therefore, they tried to tie Christianity in with Greek thought and said such things that implied we cannot trust Paul. We can only trust those writers who identify Christianity with Greek thought. We must take the Gospels, particularly the Sermon on the Mount, and go back to the simple teachings of Jesus.

This, however, is absolutely false. When John wrote his gospel, he was not identifying Christianity with Greek thought. Not one line in the New Testament gives even a hint that John knew anything about Greek thought, despite having lived in a Roman-controlled, Hellenized (Greek) culture. John, you remember, and his brother James, were simple fishermen and did not know or study anything about Greek thought.

In John's lifetime, Palestine was an occupied country. John was not a scholar, had not gone to Athens to study, as the apostle Paul had, under Gamaliel. John was simply identifying the doctrine of the Word with Old Testament doctrine—the Hebrew doctrine, if you please. He was identifying Jesus Christ with the Old Testament doctrine of the creating

Word. That is not Greek thought, but rather antedates Greek thought by thousands of years.

In the book of Genesis, for example, we read,

> In the beginning God created the heaven and the earth. And the earth was without form, and void; and darkness was upon the face of the deep. And the Spirit of God moved upon the face of the waters. And God said, Let there be light: and there was light. And God saw the light, that it was good: and God divided the light from the darkness. And God called the light Day, and the darkness he called Night. And the evening and the morning were the first day.
>
> 1:1–5

Here we have from the beginning the voice of eternal wisdom, the creating voice of God. He commanded, and it came forth. He spoke, and it was done. It was the commanding voice of God that brought things into being, as it is written, He "[upheld] all things by the word of his power" (Hebrews 1:3). Everything in creation is built upon the foundation of this creating voice.

Along with this, we have the speaking voice.

When we come to the speaking voice of God in His universe, it is this that continually holds all things together. It is in Him all things are held together and not by anything adhesive or by law, but held together by the voice of God.

The apostle John was identifying Jesus Christ with the old Hebrew doctrine of creating wisdom, the spoken word into the creating voice that created all things, and he was not associating it at all with Greek thought, though he had every intention that the Greeks would comprehend what he wrote.

In reading the church fathers, you will see that they believed this. They saw in Jesus Christ the incarnation of this ancient afflatus, this brightness of the everlasting light, the unspotted mirror of the power of God, an image of His goodness entering into souls, making them prophets and friends of God.

What was it that entered into those souls, making them prophets? It is written that it was the Spirit of Christ speaking. The book of Psalms testifies that the Spirit speaking through David makes him sometimes sound like the Messiah: "My God, my God, why hast thou forsaken me? Why art thou so far from helping me?" (Psalm 22:1). David was writing, of course, but it was the Messiah, the Spirit of the Messiah, the ancient wisdom of God that was speaking through the man David.

I am reminded of the passage that says, "And the light shineth in darkness; and the darkness comprehended it not" (John 1:5). The darkness cannot prevail against the light, and so we identify the Hebrew doctrine of the ancient and eternal wisdom with the New Testament.

The apostle Paul taught that this distinguished Greek thought from Hebrew doctrine. Other apostles may not have known how to do that, but Paul could because he was well educated, having studied the Hebrew Scriptures as well as Greek philosophy. The others were forced to stay by the text while Paul could speak about Greek thought. He said, "For the Jews require a sign, and the Greeks seek after wisdom: But we preach Christ crucified, unto the Jews a stumblingblock, and unto the Greeks foolishness; but unto them which are called, both Jews and Greeks, Christ the power of God, and the wisdom of God" (1 Corinthians 1:22–24).

In that same chapter, Paul writes, "But of him are ye in Christ Jesus, who of God is made unto us wisdom, and righteousness, and sanctification, and redemption" (1 Corinthians 1:30). He distinguished sharply in those first two chapters Greek thought from the Hebrew doctrine of the Messiah and said,

> And I, brethren, when I came to you, came not with excellency of speech or of wisdom, declaring unto you the testimony of God. For I determined not to know any thing among you, save Jesus Christ, and him crucified. And I was with you in weakness, and in fear, and in much trembling. And my speech and my preaching was not with enticing words of man's wisdom, but in demonstration of the Spirit and of power: That your faith should not stand in the wisdom of men, but in the power of God.
>
> 1 Corinthians 2:1–5

The apostle Paul was writing to the Corinthians. At the time, their city, Corinth, was known as an academic city with many philosophers, intellectuals, and scholars who wrote with an understanding of how they were thinking and how to challenge their Greek thought with the Hebrew doctrine of wisdom.

Always remember that whenever we begin to equate Christianity with any current philosophy, however ancient and honorable its roots, Christianity loses its power immediately. The apostle Paul steadfastly refused to do that.

Paul distinguished the doctrine of Christ, the wisdom of God, from the mere Greek use of *logos* as "word," but saw what the apostle John saw: that the doctrine of the divine Logos, the Word, was none other than the wisdom of God.

18

I would say that some of those old Greeks got pretty close to it sometimes, but they were limited by their own human reason and logic. The wisdom taught by the Hebrews was larger than any culture and could never be contained or explained.

☙ SHALL WISDOM CRY ALOUD? ❧

Shall Wisdom cry aloud,
And not her speech be heard?
The voice of God's eternal Word,
Deserves it no regard?

Isaac Watts

2

Christ, the Wisdom of God

10 · 6 · 25

O Christ, Thou most glorious Ancient of Days, pour into my soul that which will enable me to see Thee as Thou wouldst have me to see Thee. Let me go beyond the sacred page, and for the glory of Thy unveiling, let me see Thee as Thou art and love Thee as Thou dost deserve. Amen.

The Hebrew doctrine of the wisdom of God is a critical aspect in understanding God's wisdom. I want to focus in this chapter on the truth that Jesus Christ is the wisdom of God, the incarnate Word.

Some believe that the New Testament writers based their teaching on Greek philosophy. But the truth is, it is Hebrew and not Greek that defines this wisdom of God. The apostle Paul said, in fact, that he rejected the Greek ideas and presented to them Jesus Christ, crucified, the Messiah. He taught that Jesus Christ is the fulfillment of the ancient Hebrew doctrine of eternal wisdom out of which came all things, and that His work is more than jewels and silver.

Look at some Scripture from the Old Testament and then compare with the New Testament.

> Wisdom hath builded her house, she hath hewn out her seven pillars: She hath killed her beasts; she hath mingled her wine; she hath also furnished her table. She hath sent forth her maidens: she crieth upon the highest places of the city, Whoso is simple, let him turn in hither: as for him that wanteth understanding, she saith to him, Come, eat of my bread, and drink of the wine which I have mingled. Forsake the foolish, and live; and go in the way of understanding.
>
> Proverbs 9:1–6

Compare that with the New Testament:

> And Jesus answered and spake unto them again by parables, and said, the kingdom of heaven is like unto a certain king, which made a marriage for his son, and sent forth his servants to call them that were bidden to the wedding: and they would not come. Again, he sent forth other servants, saying, Tell them which are bidden, Behold, I have prepared my dinner: my oxen and my fatlings are killed, and all things are ready: come unto the marriage.
>
> Matthew 22:1–4

Comparing these passages, it is almost word-for-word from the book of Proverbs. This indicates that the Lord Jesus Christ literally was the incarnation and the fulfillment of this voice of wisdom carried out to the sons of men. He is not only the Lord and head of the church; He is that, but that is not all. He is not only the coming King of kings and King of the world; He is that, but that is not all.

He is the Enlightener, the Illuminator, the Quickener, the Anointer. In every way, he is the absolute incarnation of wisdom as defined by the Hebrew doctrine of wisdom.

How can we begin to understand and appreciate this?

In my opinion, a good hymnbook is the best commentary on the Scriptures. Isaac Watts and Charles Wesley, just to name two, were better commentators than some of the commentaries that have been written over the last half-century. Just get their hymns, read and study them. They did not stick material in to fill the space the way many do today to make it rhyme. Everything was thought out carefully and set down and cut like jewels. Charles Wesley's commentary on the Scriptures is done in his hymns. Not the whole Scriptures, but the salient passages from the beginning of Genesis on through to Malachi. All the outstanding passages of Scripture, instead of preaching a sermon on them, he wrote a hymn. And what hymns they are!

I get more information and more light by reading his hymns than all of the so-called commentaries of today.

Let me emphasize the fact that Christ is our Enlightener.

For example, when Isaac Watts wrote his hymn "I'll Praise My Maker," he included the phrase "The Lord pours eyesight on the blind." Can you conceive of anything more wonderful? Can you think of a man blind from birth? Then God pours eyesight on the blind. He is a Bringer of eyesight. He is a mind Regulator, and he is all that. He is an Enlightener, so when the Scripture says, "The people which sat in darkness saw great light; and to them which sat in the region and shadow of death light is sprung up" (Matthew

4:16), they are quoting from the old Hebrew doctrine of eternal wisdom.

The Wisdom that created all things, which was God, and was with God, and out of which came all things that are had all the attributes of deity. This is the Hebrew doctrine of wisdom as laid forth in Old Testament Scripture.

Many hymn writers, I have noticed, make wisdom to include the attributes of God. Not all, certainly, but many that you could not give to anyone else: an understanding spirit, holy, One only. Then you have the famous Hebrew doctrine, "Hear, O Israel: the Lord our God is one Lord" (Deuteronomy 6:4). There is His sovereignty, having all power. There is His omnipotence, overseeing all things. There is His omniscience, all understanding. There is His all-knowledge, His holiness. It is the breath of the power of God and a pure influence flowing from the glory of the Almighty. For the brightness of the everlasting light, He is the unspotted mirror of the power of God and the image of His goodness.

It is so inspiring to go through many of these hymns and see how they are true to the Hebrew doctrine of wisdom as they present the Lord Jesus Christ.

Then in the New Testament, we find the apostle Paul's prayer for the Colossians: "For this cause we also, since the day we heard it, do not cease to pray for you, and to desire that ye might be filled with the knowledge of his will in all wisdom and spiritual understanding" (1:9). This is in complete harmony with the Hebrew doctrine of wisdom. This flows throughout many of the great hymns of the church.

What would wisdom and spiritual understanding, for example, make out of man? Would the man filled with wisdom and spiritual understanding write cheap poetry? I would certainly hope not. What then does he do? Walk around in a brown robe and pull loose from the world, hiding in a cloister or an ivory tower? Absolutely not.

What is the purpose then of this baptism of the ancient wisdom of God into the heart of a man? The old wisdom man said it was to make a man a friend of God. Paul said, "That ye might walk worthy of the Lord unto all pleasing, being fruitful in every good work, and increasing in the knowledge of God; strengthened with all might, according to his glorious power, unto all patience and longsuffering with joyfulness" (Colossians 1:10–11). This is the practical meaning of this infusion of divine wisdom into the man walking with God.

I must point out that this is not a once- or twice-a-year event. It is not like taking out one of Mozart's musical pieces, playing it for friends on a special occasion, and then putting it away until the next time. Rather, it is practical, hard, and sound. You can hear it, and it means something. It means something to the whole church of Christ. If we only saw this and understood it.

Again, quoting from the *Wisdom of Solomon*: "For into a malicious soul, wisdom shall not enter; nor dwell in the body that is subject unto sin" (1:4). Wisdom, according to this ancient wisdom, will not enter into a malicious soul, but is poured out upon a man who is pure and will not come upon any person subject to sin. The inner heart and the outer body both have to be clean.

We have to be right inwardly and outwardly before we can have this afflatus, this anointing that Paul prayed for the Colossians. William Cowper is quoted as saying: "Wisdom and goodness are twin-born, one heart must hold both sisters, never seen apart."

If you are going to have wisdom in your heart, you have to take the other sister along, which is goodness. Wisdom and goodness are twin-born. One heart must hold both sisters, and they are never seen apart. When the Lord redeems man and saves him, He sets him apart, and not only to go to heaven at last and escape hell. This frightful effort to get across that bridge and escape hell would be funny if it were not so tragic. The purpose of God in redemption is not just to save us *from* hell. The purpose of God in redemption is to save us *unto* heaven.

To be totally saved, He has to save us from something in order to save us unto something. We are saved from sin, which is the negative side. We are saved unto holiness, which is the positive side. We are saved from hell, but we are saved unto heaven. We are saved from the devil, but we are saved unto Christ. The teaching of the Scriptures is that we Christians are followers of the One who came into the world and claimed to be the fulfillment of all the ancient teachings of the prophets and sages and seers and men who walked with God.

We are followers of the One who claimed He was with the Father in the beginning and that out of His bosom flow all wisdom, knowledge, and light. Jesus did not hesitate to say, "I am the light of the world" (John 8:12). He did not hesitate to refer to wisdom when quoting a prophet. Jesus used the word *wisdom*, and told others to look to Him for that ancient breath of God, that ancient wisdom.

The most educated person today, with several PhDs, may not know this. He may know many things, more than I will ever know, but there are some things he will never know by going through the process of education. Unless he knows

Christ, he does not know that ancient wisdom that was with the Father and that stood up before the world as Christ himself. He must be introduced to Him by the incarnation, the atonement, the resurrection, and the new birth. This is the only way that eternal wisdom taught by the ancient Hebrews can come into a person's life.

Reading one of Charles Spurgeon's sermons, I came across a very interesting phrase. He said, in effect, let a man build himself a house on the hillside under the shadow of Calvary and he will be wiser than the seven sages of antiquity. We do not have to stand up before the most intelligent of this world and apologize. The only thing we have to apologize for is our sin.

When we deal with our sin, repent, and the Lord has taken our sin away, we are as wise as the angels and as discrete and as knowing as the seraphs before the throne, for we have an afflatus of that wisdom.

This eternal wisdom as taught by the Hebrews will not teach you mathematics, science, chemistry, or English literature. All of those are within the confines of man's wisdom. However, this eternal wisdom will teach you something vaster, wiser, deeper, grander, and more wonderful. It will baptize you into that light, that wonderful light. This is the breath of the power of God, the pure influence flowing from the glory of the Almighty. This wisdom is the brightness of the everlasting Light, the unspotted mirror of the power of God, and the image of His goodness.

If I may add a personal testimony, I would rather have the baptism of this light in my spirit than pastor the biggest church in the world and be known around the world. Anyone can get to that place with man's wisdom. I want to go beyond man's wisdom and experience the eternal wisdom that can only come as an afflatus from on high.

This is why the apostle Paul said, "That I might know him, and the power of his resurrection, and the fellowship of his sufferings" (Philippians 3:10). I believe that is why the apostle Paul pressed on to know him better and better, because in doing that, he was going back to the fountain of everything.

❧ IMMORTAL, INVISIBLE, GOD ONLY WISE ❧

Immortal, invisible, God only wise,
In light inaccessible, hid from our eyes,
Most blessed, most glorious, the Ancient of Days,
Almighty, victorious, Thy great name we praise.
Walter C. Smith

3

The Effect of
Poured-Out Wisdom

*O Wisdom, the incarnate Christ, fill my heart with
desires that please Thee and show to the world around
me Thy amazing grace. May my life today reflect the
glory of eternal wisdom and let me never be satisfied
with my limited wisdom and knowledge. Amen.*

In the Old Testament and in old Hebrew literature, there
is a doctrine called the doctrine of eternal wisdom. It
is the Hebrew concept that says somewhere out there
is God and with God and beside God and yet being God,
there is an afflatus, a fullness of wisdom of word and idea
and concept and expression. We also find this teaching in
the New Testament.

David expressed it well: "By the word of the Lord were the heavens made; and all the host of them by the breath of his mouth" (Psalm 33:6). This is the Hebrew concept of wisdom. It is quite different from the idea that God made everything by hand. David is writing this about one thousand years before the birth of Christ. In the books of Proverbs and Ecclesiastes, we find the same idea: that eternal wisdom, which gave birth to everything.

Also in the book of Job, written at least nineteen hundred years before Christ—most think it is the oldest book of the Bible—Job believed the doctrine of the eternal Word, the eternal wisdom. This teaching of the eternal wisdom in the Old Testament is consistent with the New Testament writers.

Solomon believed it and wrote of it in his Proverbs and in the book of Ecclesiastes a thousand years before the birth of Christ.

The teaching of the Old Testament on this is that there was a creative impulse, that God had an idea, a thought, and out of that came everything.

> For I know the thoughts that I think toward you, saith the Lord, thoughts of peace, and not of evil, to give you an expected end.
>
> Jeremiah 29:11

> For my thoughts are not your thoughts, neither are your ways my ways, saith the Lord.
>
> Isaiah 55:8

According to Hebrew doctrine, this eternal wisdom, which was with the Son, was the created fountain out of which everything came. The rabbis, the old church fathers, the men of God who lived and studied the Scriptures, believed this. John picked up on it, not from the Greeks, but from the Hebrews, when he wrote, "In the beginning was the Word . . ."

The consistency of this teaching reveals to us the hand of God. This is what God wants us to know, and He desires to share His wisdom with His creation.

The apostle Paul also teaches the same thing:

> Who is the image of this invisible God, the firstborn of every creature: For by him were all things created, that are in heaven, and that are in earth, visible and invisible, whether they be thrones, or dominions, or principalities, or powers: all things were created by him, and for him: And he is before all things, and by him all things consist.
>
> Colossians 1:15–17

The emphasis we find in Paul's writings was that this was the flowering of the Old Testament teaching. It flowered over into the New Testament and so Jesus Christ came, who was himself that eternal wisdom, took upon him the form of a man, was incarnated in mortal flesh, and walked among men. I find it interesting that as a twelve-year-old, Jesus put the doctors of religion to flight and asked questions they could not answer while he answered every question they asked Him.

Paul puts it correctly when he says, "For the Jews require a sign, and the Greeks seek after wisdom" (1 Corinthians 1:22). Paul firmly believed that Jesus Christ is both the power of God and the wisdom of God, and in Him all the treasures of wisdom and knowledge are hidden away. Apart from Jesus Christ, God's wisdom can never be accessed, and it is this wisdom that enables us to be what God created and redeemed us to be.

This beautiful doctrine of the presence of something, the old mystics called *Sophia*, which means "maid of wisdom." They said the Lord by wisdom had founded the earth, by understanding He had established the heavens (Proverbs 3:19), and has established the world by His wisdom and stretched out the heavens by His discretion (Jeremiah 10:12). How can you understand that apart from Jesus Christ being the wisdom of God?

As I look at this and think about it, I see two triads: the earth, the heavens, and the world founded and established, stretched out by wisdom, understanding, and discretion.

I take this to be a hint of the Trinity. This is Old Testament doctrine: here is the earth, founded by wisdom; the heavens, established by understanding; the world, which was stretched out by discretion.

In reading Job, Ecclesiastes, or Proverbs you will find that this wisdom, understanding, and discretion was a person. This person was someone you wooed and won. It was something—an afflatus, a holy oil—God poured out on His people. The descriptions vary, but you find they are all pointing to the same thing. David said, "By the word of the Lord were the heavens made; and all the host of them by the breath of his mouth" (Psalm 33:6).

I referred in a previous chapter to a book called the *Wisdom of Solomon* and pointed out very carefully that this is not an inspired book in the sense that Psalms or Proverbs or Isaiah are inspired. It represents, however, the good word. I quote from this book as I would quote from the church fathers down through the years. It is not an inspired book, but it is a book that helps us understand this doctrine of wisdom from the Hebrew standpoint. It is included in the apocryphal books, which are not included in the sacred canon of Scripture.

Another book along this line is *Ecclesiasticus,* not to be confused with Ecclesiastes. This book was written about two hundred years before Christ and gives the beliefs and teachings of the early fathers, taught by the inspired Scriptures. This is included in the apocryphal books.

Here is what he said:

> All wisdom cometh from the Lord, and is with him for ever. Who can number the sand of the sea, and the drops of rain, and the days of eternity? Who can find out the height of heaven, and the breadth of the earth, and the deep, and wisdom? Wisdom hath been created before all things, and the understanding of prudence from everlasting.
>
> *Ecclesiasticus* 1:1–4

We do not have to concern ourselves about what is happening out in the world, because all wisdom comes from the Lord and is with Him forever and "Who can number the sand of the sea, and the drops of rain, and the days of eternity?" (*Ecclesiasticus* 1:2). All that is happening out in our world is no challenge whatsoever to the wisdom of God. Nothing the world can do could ever in the least compromise this wisdom of God.

Go to nature, for example. We wonder how the wild bird finds its way north in the spring and south in the fall. We are amazed how the orchard oriole and the Baltimore oriole manage to build their beautiful swinging nests. Then we are amazed at how the honeybee finds its way across the meadow to its hive. It is here that we wonder about what some refer to as instinct. I can quote several verses where it says God poured wisdom out upon His creation, and I believe what the bee has is a divine touch from the hand that made it.

God made the bee, did He not? God also made the birds, and even says in one place, you are dumber than the ox that knows its master, the created bird that knows her nest; and my people do not know, neither do they consider (Isaiah 1:3). Man, made in the image of God, lost the wisdom, but the very creation around him has that wisdom.

That is why I do not worry about the universe. It will be all right in the long run. I believe God has poured out wisdom upon all His creation, so that everything works as it should because God made it that way.

Many people are worried about the universe without remembering that they had nothing whatsoever to do with the creation of it. I believe if you cannot create it, you cannot fix it, and it is best left in God's hands.

This doctrine of eternal wisdom was incarnated in Jesus Christ, which is why it is so hard to understand. This is the root and base of it all; it is the old Hebrew doctrine that God is wisdom. We sing about this:

GOD IS LOVE! HIS MERCY BRIGHTENS

God is love! His mercy brightens
All the path in which we rove;
Bliss He wakes, and woe He lightens:
God is wisdom! God is love!

John Bowring

Jesus Christ was the incarnation of this wisdom of God. I challenge you to do a bit of research, and I am sure you will be enlightened, illuminated, and delighted, perhaps even ravished, as you see how before Mary ever gave birth, before the baby Jesus wailed His tiny protest to the world in Bethlehem's manger, what the theologians call pre-incarnation times, Jesus Christ was the Wisdom of the Father.

He was of one substance with the Father, equal with the Father, as ancient as the Father, eternal with the Father, having all the attributes of the Father. He was the Father's outgoing, the Father's expression, and that is what the book of John says, "In the beginning was the Word . . ."

ERE GOD HAD BUILT THE MOUNTAINS

Ere God had built the mountains,
Or raised the fruitful hills;
Before he fill'd the fountains
That feed the running rills;
In me from everlasting,
The wonderful I Am,
Found pleasures never wasting,
And Wisdom is my name.
                    William Cowper

4

Lessons from the Doctrine of Eternal Wisdom

O God, Thou Eternal Wisdom, May I embrace that which you have created me for, and may out of my life flow the thanks and praise you so desire. Let me live my life by the wisdom of Thy Son, the Lord Jesus Christ. Amen.

Greek students have had an awful time translating the words of John because John went so far beyond the average, and it takes a lot of sanctified imagination to understand him. Most today do not have a sanctified imagination, so they settle for a footnote, and that is as far as they go.

In examining this doctrine of eternal wisdom, what do we learn? How does this affect Christianity today? If it does not affect my life today, of what value is it and why should I spend time pursuing it?

In our day, we have degraded Christianity to be a kind of soft vaccine against hell and sin. We gather people, stick them with a religious needle, and say, "If you just accept Jesus you will not go to hell, you will go to heaven when you die. Keep living as well as you can, and when you die you'll go to heaven." Many are preaching what I refer to as a kind of lifeboat salvation, and even the songs today reflect that idea.

Certainly, this is an inadequate concept of Christianity. The purpose of God in redeeming men was not to save them from hell only, but to save them to worship, and to allow them to be born into that eternal wisdom that was with the Father, which is synonymous with that eternal life that was with the Father and was revealed unto men.

One of the most astounding passages from the apostle John is 1 John 1:1–3:

> That which was from the beginning, which we have heard, which we have seen with our eyes, which we have looked upon, and our hands have handled, of the Word of life. . . . That which we have seen and heard declare we unto you . . . our fellowship is with the Father, and with his Son Jesus Christ.

Through the mouth of this man of God, the Holy Spirit spoke of a holy and happy communion, light and life and the Word; the Word was life, and the Light was the light of men, and in Him was life. Only the Holy Spirit can reveal that to you, but as we meditate upon the concept, it opens up our hearts to what Christianity is all about.

This eternal life is all one because it is Jesus Christ our Lord, and it touches us unless, of course, we have been brainwashed to the point where we cannot think this way. The Greeks sought after this and could not find it, and Paul explained it to them in Acts 17:22–24:

> Then Paul stood in the midst of Mars' hill, and said, Ye men of Athens, I perceive that in all things ye are too superstitious. For as I passed by, and beheld your devotions, I found an altar with this inscription, TO THE UNKNOWN GOD. Whom therefore ye ignorantly worship, him declare I unto you. God that made the world and all things therein, seeing that he is Lord of heaven and earth, dwelleth not in temples made with hands.

Nothing is more unbecoming, in my view, than for Christian preachers to become nasty and tough and say a great deal of harsh things about the great philosophers and the ancient religions. They did what they could with the life they had. I wonder if we can say the same thing about ourselves today?

For instance, Heraclitus of Ephesus (c. 535–c. 475 BC), 600 years before Christ, probably never heard of Solomon, or the book of Proverbs or Job, and probably never read a Psalm in his life. Somewhere in his dreaming and crying after the Most High God, he thought his way through to the idea of eternal life and that Word out of which everything came, and then gave the Greeks the doctrine of "the word," which Plato and others brought to perfection.

They tried their best, but fell short of discovering that eternal wisdom, which was fulfilled in Jesus Christ.

In the human quest, the Jews sought after righteousness, the Greeks sought after wisdom, and the religionists sought after redemption. Paul was preaching Jesus, and said to these people that he had news for them: "This Jesus, whom I preach unto you, is Christ" (Acts 17:3). The Greek scholars tell us that what he said was that He was made unto us wisdom, righteousness, sanctification, and redemption. What Paul was saying was that Jesus Christ *is* our wisdom, our righteousness, our sanctification, and our redemption.

This is what we call ancient wisdom, which the Greeks and the Hebrews before them talked about as uncreated and yet somehow created, but is it any stranger than the passage that says, "The Word was with God, and the Word was God" (John 1:1)? Which was it? With God, or was it God?

Actually, He was both, so we say that same truth applies to the ancient idea that there is a fountain of wisdom, the womb out of which was born all things that exist. I can live in this world believing and not worry about it, not getting into too many intellectual jams because this world is beautifully put together.

How does this really impact our lives today? What do we learn from all this?

First, we learn that the universe is basically spiritual.

Lucretius (99 BC–55 BC) wrote his famous "The Nature of Things," saying that there were atoms, and they were little hard square blocks like dice, and everything was made up of these little square blocks. As far as I know, he was the first to popularize the idea of the atom.

Approximately two thousand years later, they discovered Lucretius was wrong. He said everything was made up of atoms, which was true. But he said those atoms were square blocks, hard as diamonds. He was wrong because modern scientific technique has discovered that these tiny little blocks were not hard blocks at all but embodied bits of energy and if you keep breaking them down you will find exactly nothing at all.

Therefore, the modern idea of the atom coincides perfectly with the Old Testament idea of creation: that all things come out of the Spirit, and if you go back far enough, you come to the Spirit. Things are basically spiritual.

The earth is not a solid thing with a spirit hovering over it. The earth is an emanation of spirit, and all things that are came out of a spirit. Even that Eternal Spirit, which we call God, was the incarnate form of a man, lived among us, and was so wise that He astonished men, though he had never been to school.

Second, we learn from this doctrine of the eternal wisdom that it is the source of all things and that man is a spirit ensheathed in a body. Man is not a body having a spirit; man is a spirit in a body.

How do you think of yourself? Do you think of yourself as your outer shell being you?

That is certainly not the teaching of the Bible. The Bible teaches that we are a spirit living in a body, which is vastly different. If I were a body having a spirit, I would worry about this body. I am a spirit made in the image of God; God is a spirit, and God made me spirit, and made me to live for a while in this body. I think it was William Jennings Bryan who referred to our body as a "temple of clay," and he hit the thing right on the head.

The great thing about you is not your body. It is not the house you live in or the car you drive. The most awesome and awe-inspiring thing about you is your spirit.

41

God made the angels spirits and made everything else flesh. He made man greater than all by compounding flesh and spirit so that man is a spirit, which has a fleshly tabernacle to dwell in. Keep in mind that all things came of spirit, and Jesus Christ was incarnated. He was that eternal wisdom, and man is a spirit ensheathed in a body. That determines your values. That decides what is valuable and what is not. Our difficulty is in our not knowing what is really valuable.

The truth of "the Word was made flesh" stands as a warning lest we forget who we are. It stands as a rebuke to us for living as animals, for living as people of one world, when God made us for two; living for time, when God made us for eternity.

Solomon says in Proverbs, "So are the ways of every one that is greedy of gain; which taketh away the life of the owners thereof. Wisdom crieth without; she uttered her voice in the streets" (1:19–20). This is nothing less than the voice of Jesus, the voice of the Holy Spirit (Proverbs 1:21–27).

This wisdom teaches us that we are not animals. God made us a spirit and gave us a body to live in so we could cart that spirit around. It is an insult if we live as animals, if we live as if we belong to time alone.

The characteristics of the men of the world are that they worry right down to the last moment about their property. They walk about on earth thinking about their cars and how big the tailgate is. We are so obsessed with clothing and outward appearance, things that do not last.

God help us that we should be like this. Instead of soaring and cooing like a dove, we find ourselves down in the garbage heap digging like a buzzard. That is when we boil Christianity down to human reason and logic. We cut the foundation out from under it with our materialistic theology and our final approach to things.

Go out in your yard tonight and look up at God's stars and say, "I am part of the everlasting universe, and I will not respond to the voice of wisdom as if I were a man made for time, for God has put eternity in my heart. Not as if I was a man made for this world, because God made me for another. Not as if I was a man of flesh, because I am a man of spirit. I will respond as a man made for eternity."

We are made in the image of God and destined to be conscious throughout eternity: an individual, a conscious entity throughout eternity, with God having given us birth out of the ancient womb of eternal wisdom, then incarnated that eternal wisdom in the power of a man and sent Him to die for us.

John Bunyan, who wrote *The Pilgrim's Progress*, reveals to us the nature of conviction from his experience. Bunyan was under conviction of the Holy Spirit for sin and it was an overwhelming experience.

Bunyan lived in the days when Christianity was not easy like it is today. He got under such blistering conviction that he was convinced he was going to hell, that one day as he was walking down the street in deep despair, he noticed a dog walking down the street and he cried out to God, *"O God, I wish I were that dog, then I could die and be no more, but I've got to face Thee in the judgment."*

It was not long before God straightened John Bunyan out and saved him. We must get away from this idea that salvation is simply saying you believe in Jesus as your Savior. We must come to the place of understanding that Christianity is a result of divine wisdom flowing into a person's life.

☙ THY WAYS, O LORD, WITH WISE DESIGN ❧

Thy ways, O Lord, with wise design
Are framed upon Thy throne above,
And every dark and bending line
Meets in the center of Thy love.

Ambrose Serle

5

Christianity Flows
Out of God's Wisdom

*O Christ, the eternal wisdom of God, I give myself
completely to Thee and turn my back on my own understanding and trust Thee completely. May Thy wisdom
flow into me and out to the world around me, creating
in me a vessel for Thy glory. Amen.*

The apostle Paul made it very clear that his preaching
was not of man's wisdom but a demonstration of
the Holy Spirit and power. In this, Paul insisted that,
as Christians, our faith should not stand in the wisdom of
man, but in the power of God.

Lest anyone should misunderstand, he said,

Your faith should not stand in the wisdom of men, but in
the power of God. Howbeit we speak wisdom among them

that are perfect: yet not the wisdom of this world, nor of the princes of this world, that come to nought: But we speak the wisdom of God in a mystery, even the hidden wisdom, which God ordained before the world unto our glory.

1 Corinthians 2:5–7

Paul also said,

For after that in the wisdom of God the world by wisdom knew not God, it pleased God by the foolishness of preaching to save them that believe. For the Jews require a sign, and the Greeks seek after wisdom: But we preach Christ crucified, unto the Jews a stumblingblock, and unto the Greeks foolishness; but unto them which are called, both Jews and Greeks, Christ the power of God, and the wisdom of God.

1 Corinthians 1:21–24

We need to understand what Paul is talking about here. His emphasis was that the Jews wanted power, the Greeks wanted wisdom, and Paul was insisting that Christ is both: the power of God and the wisdom of God.

Throughout his writings, the apostle Paul consistently points out that Christianity is a divine thing in the sense that ordinary created things are not divine. Christianity flowed out of God's wisdom. Christianity is not a creation of the human mind, and because it is not, it cannot be explained by the human mind. Neither psychology nor philosophy can explain Christianity. It can, however, explain denominationalism and all that we see around us that passes for Christianity today.

"We speak," Paul said, "the wisdom of God in a mystery, even the hidden wisdom, which God ordained before the world unto our glory" (1 Corinthians 2:7). This cannot be explained by the mind of man because it was not created by the mind of man.

Whatever one mind creates an equal mind can explain. What no mind created, no mind can explain, and when psychology tries to explain Christianity, what it is explaining is not biblical Christianity. Jesus, when He was on earth, sometimes spoke in a parable. Those parables could be understood only by the elect, those infused with divine wisdom.

This mystery of Christianity is a parable, which can be explained not at all by the mind, but only be grasped as the Holy Spirit illuminates the heart. So that Christianity cannot be promoted except by eternal wisdom and power. You can promote religion without divine wisdom and power. You can promote your denomination. You can promote and build up your church numerically and financially, but in these ways, you cannot promote true Christianity.

Personally, I am devoted and dedicated to Christianity, which cannot be promoted except by eternal wisdom and power. Our Lord said, "For I will give you a mouth and wisdom, which all your adversaries shall not be able to gainsay nor resist" (Luke 21:15). If we imagine this is simply religious talk, go forward a few years to the sixth chapter of Acts, where Stephen is preaching to the Jews and it says, "They were not able to resist the wisdom and the spirit by which he spake" (Acts 6:10).

I believe the compelling need of this hour is for Christians to receive from God a baptism of eternal wisdom, the creative wisdom of God. Lacking this, the church is blind. An ancient proverb goes something like this: Though the blind man holds a lantern, yet he will fall into the ditch, for a lantern held by a blind man might as well be an old boot. It takes eyes to use a lantern, and so the church, when it does not have eyes, can have all kinds of teachers and teaching and promoters and promotion, but nevertheless it will go into the ditch, because lacking this creative wisdom, the church is blind.

Some in the church try to make up for this blindness by scholarship. In my opinion, scholarship is but a glass eye. It looks like an eye, feels like an eye, and to the uninitiated, it is an eye, but essentially, there is just one little thing wrong: you cannot see with that eye.

The evangelical church wavers today because it has burst out in two directions: One, in the direction of entertainment and pleasure for the like-minded ones. The other, in the direction of scholarship for the serious-minded. This is the new evangelicalism of today. An effort to do by scholarship what can only be done by wisdom and power. It is a glass eye trying to see.

This may sound strange, but the day will come when the church of Christ will see this, and increasing numbers of gifted and able men will teach this and we will break out into a new kind of Christianity. By that I mean something new from what we have now, new in the sense that it is biblical.

Years ago, I discovered a writer by the name of Francesco Petrarch (1304–1374), known as the father of humanism as we understand it today. He wrote a book that intrigued me entitled *On My Own Ignorance*. After reading it, I discovered he was not writing on his own ignorance at all, rather he was writing in defense of his knowledge. However, we really do not know very much these days.

Right now, the church is taken up with science, psychology, philosophy, and even theology. There is hardly a field of human learning in which I do not have at least a certain amount of curiosity, but there is not a field where I am proficient. To quote this man, Francesco Petrarch, from his book, "I am a man who is a lover of learning rather than one who has got much of it." He confessed that he had not gotten much, but what he had he liked. I think I can identify with that.

All the great minds who ever had any kind of a mind knew they did not know very much, and, in fact, could not know very much. That is why God does not permit salvation to rely on the great scholar. In our time, evangelicalism is busy stirring up a great deal of dust and trouble trying to show that we can meet the challenges of our day by Christian scholarship. We could, but evangelicalism is not producing illuminated thinkers, men with the divine afflatus of wisdom, that mysterious something, which was hidden, but has been revealed for our glory and the end of the age to come.

Scholars these days are a dime a dozen. Shake a scholar and you get a great many things that fall out. Shaking a scholar is like shaking a ten-year-old boy's pants after he goes to bed. Pick them up by the hems and shake them out, and you will be surprised, possibly even horrified, about what drops to the floor. Just about anything is likely to drop out, from a half-dead toad to a half-eaten sandwich, and up and down the scale. Shake a scholar and you will find all sorts of information falling out in all directions.

I have come to one conclusion, though: He who memorizes Scripture and has it on the tip of his tongue so that he can quote it, but does not obey it, is like a herdsman counting other people's cattle. He is busy concerning himself with others' cattle while he has not one heifer of his own. That could describe the average scholar today. They try to accomplish by intellectual effort what can only be done by divine wisdom and power.

We are trying to meet the needs of the hour by our own brains and scholarship, but it will never work, because a scholar and an illuminated thinker are two different people. The two might be the same, I suppose, by definition. But the scholar is not generally an illuminated thinker because that is not his job. His job is to classify information, whether it's about Lincoln or uranium or any number of facts concerning history or geology. That is his business, but not to press through to a mental and inward illumination.

I must allow that the scholar could be an illuminated thinker if he has a baptism of divine wisdom, but just as a man could have red hair and play a violin, there would be no relation between his red hair and his violin. Today we have all kinds of Bible teachers and scholars and thinkers. We are followers of leaders, and our trouble is that the leaders are not always divinely illuminated.

Take one man, give him eyes, and a voice to speak, and ninety-nine blind men can follow him rather safely. If this man is an illuminated man, the ninety-nine blind men can follow him and stay out of trouble as long as he keeps making himself heard. But it has become obvious over the last quarter of a century that our leaders are not illuminated men. They say some convincing words, and everyone runs after them, but everyone is headed in the wrong direction. We have ignored the fact that Christianity has a divine source; it is divinely ordained, divinely given, and it cannot be humanly explained. It can only be promoted by divine wisdom and power. Except we have that divine wisdom and power, we are blind leaders of the blind.

What I am praying for is that God Almighty would come upon this generation of Christians and make them dissatisfied with the cold, humanistic, intellectual evangelicalism of our time, and make them so thirsty for an afflatus of divine wisdom and power that they press through and receive that baptism.

Do not misunderstand me here. I believe some great scholars have gone on to be great illuminated men. For example, Moses was a great scholar. He was learned in all the wisdom of Egypt and brought up in the court as the son of Pharaoh's daughter. He was given every advantage in learning, but before God could use him to lead Israel out of Egypt, He took him to the burning bush in order that he might be illuminated for the job. The Lord was not going to trust Israel to a man with a head full of Egyptian learning until he illuminated that man. Until he experienced the afflatus of divine wisdom and power, he could not be used of God.

Another scholar we hear from in the New Testament was the man Paul. Following his conversion, he disappeared for three years somewhere down in Arabia. He was not learning from the Arabians, but was hiding out, seeking something from God. When he went back, he had what he lacked before. He was a scholar, but he went on to be an illuminated man, a man who knew divine wisdom and power, something beyond the intellect.

This is what I am attempting to focus on. The Bible teaches in both the Old and the New Testaments that there is a hidden wisdom, which does not consist of facts or statistics or the classification of events. It is a timeless, uncreated sea into which men are plunged by the Holy Spirit. Sometimes it is conceived as God the Father, sometimes as the Son of

God, sometimes as something that God created and sent out, sometimes as a woman standing at the gates of the city, crying out, "O ye simple, understand wisdom: and, ye fools, be ye of an understanding heart" (Proverbs 8:5). It is not merely intellect on fire, and that is what makes the difference.

"The mind," St. Nikephoros, the monk, said, "when it unites with the heart is filled with unspeakable joy and delight. Then a man sees that the kingdom of heaven is truly within us. Then it will teach you things which you in no other way will ever learn."

In the fall of man a dislocation took place, a separation, and man's brain was separated from his inner spirit. In redemption, the two are reunited so that the Christian man thinks with his heart, where the sinner, however learned he is, only thinks with his head. The truth of the matter is, you can think with both. You could push your mind into your heart so that you think out of your heart. If you do this with strong desire and intention, you will be full of sweetness and there will be a whole host of virtues: love, joy, and peace; and every petition of yours will be answered in the name of Jesus Christ the Lord.

This strange, yet beautiful, gracious, loving, charitable, pure thing that God wants to pour out on you, this wisdom of God is contrary to the wisdom of man. The wisdom of God is a mystery, a hidden wisdom ordained before the world began for His glory. This wisdom is Christ the power of God and the wisdom of God.

On a personal level, I desire to be more than a theologian. Theology is the wood on the altar. Elijah on the mountain cut the wood and made himself an altar. Then he prayed, and fire came down from God and set the wood on fire, burning everything and turning the tide in favor of Jehovah and against Baal.

Theology is the wood of the sacrifice; if you do not get fire on the wood, you have nothing but wood, and a pound or two of wood never bothered anybody. If Moses had seen only the pile of wood in the wilderness, he never would have turned aside to see this great sight. Fire excites interest, and when the fire fell, there was undivided interest.

❧ ALL THAT I AM I OWE TO THEE ❧

All that I am I owe to thee,
thy wisdom, Lord, has fashioned me.
I give my Maker thankful praise,
whose wondrous works my soul amaze.
The Psalter, 1912

6

The Root of Divine Wisdom

O Holy Spirit, I praise Thee through the divine wisdom that Thou hast poured into my life, enabling me to understand who I am and who Thou art and how we come together. Amen.

My observation is that we have maintained the church of Jesus Christ as an ascetic ward in the hospital and never managed to get anybody out of it. We have people in the church, tall in stature, and yet still being looked after by nurses, still being fed from a bottle, and we do not even try to make them grow. We feed them the same baby food year after year.

Some Christians have not read a decent book in the last twenty years. They have grown physically, but spiritually they are still in the hospital ward.

For the most part, Christians are not concerned; we want to go to heaven when we die, but we forget that God said, "The meek will he guide in judgment: and the meek will he teach his way" (Psalm 25:9). We forget that the meek man Moses was the man who got the law. We forget that the meek man Paul was the man who established the theology of the New Testament. We forget that when there is purity and humility, then comes illumination and light. If the people of God were truly purified, they would find their minds illuminated and they would think with their hearts.

A Pure People

Christians today have forgotten that we are to be a pure people. God means for His church to be a pure people, so pure that we are aflame with it.

Many have put Christianity down to the level of simply saying, "I accept Christ," which is supposed to set the bells ringing in heaven and scare the devil off with his tail between his legs. That is their simplified idea of Christianity.

But we forget that accepting Christ is only the beginning. Now that I have committed myself to Jesus Christ, I have also committed myself to the purity of Christ that I can only understand by an afflatus of divine wisdom flowing into my heart. It is the wisdom of God that defines for me this purity acceptable to God.

Reverence

There is also reverence. Wisdom is a loving spirit and will not tolerate blasphemy. The Spirit of the Lord fills the world.

To fear the Lord is the root of all wisdom. Reverence flows from divine wisdom.

I am appalled at the flippancy of some preachers. They can tell a joke easier than they can talk about God. It is not that I am in favor of gloom, but when we come to the things of God, there has to be a reverent approach. Sincerity, reverence, and that sense of awe before God, and if we do not have it, we will never have the baptism of wisdom and power.

Love

Following purity and reverence is love. "She, wisdom, is with all flesh according to his gift and he gave her freely to them that love him" (*Ecclesiasticus* 1:1–10). We must have a loving and sympathetic heart. We must have empathy, which is the ability to project your own self and feelings into someone else. Jesus saw the multitude and was moved with compassion. That is empathy, extending your heart to somebody else and feeling as they feel.

A hard man will never be a wise man. He may get degrees and pile up information, but he will never be a man of great wisdom, because wisdom involves a loving spirit. God, the Holy Ghost, is a loving Spirit, full of wisdom to love.

Obedience

"If thou desire wisdom, keep the commandments, and the Lord shall give her unto thee freely" (*Ecclesiasticus* 1:26). We must be courageously obedient. It is not a question of whether you want to be obedient or not. It is a matter of whether you will be obedient or be blind. The obedient Christian will be the seeing Christian. It is by obedience that we take up the cross, not by singing about the cross. By taking the cross we are obeying, and when we obey, we carry the cross. It is when the obedience of the cross comes into your life that you notice how wisdom and power are centered on the cross of Jesus Christ. "For the preaching of the cross is to them that perish foolishness; but unto us which are saved it is the power of God" (1 Corinthians 1:18).

Wisdom and power cannot be separated from the cross. If we do not obey, we blind ourselves, and we become dependent upon our own intellect, which will be in no way sufficient to teach others.

Selflessness

Another old Greek, St. Gregory, said, "True reason such as a man had in the beginning cannot be had or acquired by any man who is not first purified and become passionless." In other words, true wisdom—that is the wisdom of the mind and heart together—cannot be acquired by any man until he has first been purified and become without worldly passion. Selfishness will blind us, and as we put self on the cross, our eyes will be opened. Wisdom poured into our life will create an attitude of selflessness.

Courage

I would like to speak a bit on this matter of courage. Our trouble now is that we do not have courage.

The best example I know of courage among preachers would be John Wesley. He first started preaching before a literal artillery barrage of eggs and tomatoes. He would go out to preach with light on his face and come back with tomatoes on his shirt. Regardless of that rejection, he kept on preaching.

When he was getting along pretty well after twelve years, he made an entry in his diary, which was rather odd. He said, "I went into such and such a village last night and to my surprise, instead of the inhabitants rushing in for tomatoes and eggs they looked at me with respect. What can be the matter?"

He could not understand how it could be that this attitude among his listeners was changing, but it did change. It changed to a point that before he died, his appearance in any English village was a holiday; they gathered around him and made a celebrity out of him. That is the way it usually is. You are either a hero or a bum. They either are throwing tomatoes at you or trying to kill you with kindness. They never succeeded in killing him with either, but it took courage in that day, because they put men in jail for preaching on the streets and drove them out of the churches and cut off their mode of living. It took courage to do what John Wesley did to preach the gospel in his day.

I am reminded of what Francis Bacon once wrote: "He that hath wife and children has given hostages to fortune, for they are impediments to great enterprises, either of virtue or mischief." No man ever said a wiser thing since Solomon. A man that has a wife and children must strive to be good because his wife and children have to live, and it's the economic crock that makes all the little ones line up like an army of worms following each other around the edge of the crock for a lifetime. Nobody daresay, "I'm going to obey God, even if my wife and family die."

When John Bunyan was in prison, they sent his wife to beg him to stop preaching, and he said, "Honey, I'm sorry about this, but I've got to stay here, because God put me here, and I won't give up."

Perhaps God has something better for us in the days ahead. I do not know, but I hope it will come soon. I hope we will understand "Christ crucified . . . the wisdom of God and the power of God." I hope we will learn and do something better than Christians have in the past and will dare to seek it and push through and not make the mistake of thinking we can learn it someplace. You cannot learn wisdom. Wisdom is a gift, not some acquirement to be learned. You cannot learn the Holy Spirit, it is a gift to be received, and I pray God will raise up people with a desire to receive it.

There are several things I am praying for God to do. I want God to restore His church again—back from her captivity—restore her to her original state of devotion, worship, purity, and get us away from this attempt to prove the Bible by science. Explain Jesus Christ by bloodline, explain His virgin birth biologically. Some are even trying to explain how the blood of Jesus Christ cleanses us from sin by the chemistry of the blood! It is absolutely horrifying how we have dragged down this mysterious, heavenly, divine Christianity of Jesus Christ called Emmanuel, God with us. He came to bring it to us and said He is in the bosom of the Father, this heavenly visitor from above, shining the blazing light of eternal wisdom. He comes, and we call ourselves His followers, but have dragged Him and

His heavenly Christianity down to the place where we try to explain it.

It behooves us to stand in His holy presence, lift our eyes, raise our hands, and say, *"O Lord God, Thou knowest all things, and we trust Thee."* Instead, we think we have to *explain* everything.

If our experience can be explained by chemistry, it is not of Jesus Christ. If it can be explained by biology, it is not of Jesus Christ. If it can be analyzed by psychology, it is not of the Holy Spirit. If philosophy has a name for it, it is not Christianity. God offers us life in Christ because of His sacrifice, and with His life in us we become pure and obedient, reverent, loving, selfless, and courageous, ready to take on whatever consequences there may be.

If you are not sure of your position in Him, take a day off and seek God, wait on Him, ask Him to reveal himself and open your blinded eyes to the true light so that you will know where you are and what you are doing.

I believe it is entirely possible to live in the world and be completely illuminated and know what is going on, know who is right and who is wrong, know by the Word of God and by the illumination of the Holy Ghost so we are more than followers, we are disciples of Jesus Christ. We are followers of Him, not followers of men. We are open-eyed, clear-eyed, clear-minded in a world of wickedness and sin with everyone following everyone else.

The Holy Spirit wants to illuminate our minds and our eyes:

But the anointing which ye have received of him abideth in you, and ye need not that any man teach you: but as the same

61

anointing teacheth you of all things, and is truth, and is no lie, and even as it hath taught you, ye shall abide in him.

1 John 2:27

My concern remains: When will the church wake up to the fact that we have slipped, we have drifted, and we need to get back to our roots in Christ? Not only accepting Christ as Savior, which is primary, basic, and fundamental, but pressing on until the blessed Holy Spirit has cleansed and purified our hearts, and in humility, obedience, and courage we push our way through and receive a breath of divine wisdom from God.

In the Old Testament, we read that God had seven thousand prophets who had not bowed their knees to Baal. What I would like to know is why they were hiding? Why didn't they come out and stand up for Jehovah? Where was their courage?

Today, Christians need to learn how to worship, and instead of having all this religious claptrap and modern entertainment to hold people together, have the fire of God and the presence of the Holy Spirit, which, by the way, will be enough.

AWAKE, MY TONGUE, THY TRIBUTE BRING

Awake, my tongue, thy tribute bring
To Him who gave thee power to sing;
Praise Him who is all praise above,
The source of wisdom and of love.

John Needham

7

The True Essence
of Divine Wisdom

*I cry unto Thee, O God. Deliver me from wallowing in
my human wisdom. I seek at all cost Thy divine wisdom
that will reveal Thee to me afresh and the values that
you have established. Thy wisdom is greater to me than
all the gold in every mine in the world. Amen.*

I have been dealing with the difference between divine
wisdom and human wisdom throughout this book. The
book of Job is a gem of priceless worth. Chapter 28 is
a dramatic search for that wisdom.

It is one thing to talk about something, to have certain
mystic flights of knowledge; it is something else altogether
to get your hands on it so that it becomes practical and part
of your working life.

"Where shall wisdom be found? and where is the place of understanding?" (v. 12).

Those are two questions, but actually, they are the same question, "Where shall wisdom be found and where is the place of understanding?"

The book of Job ranks with the top pieces of literature of all time. Even those scholars who do not believe in the inspiration of the Scriptures rate Job high among them all. The difference between Job and Homer, for example, is that Job was inspired by God; others did not have that inspiration, and so we find God in Job, but we do not find God in Homer.

The twenty-eighth chapter of Job is the dramatic story of man's search for a great treasure. The Holy Spirit literally passed His hand over the world and made this chapter a summation of the long search for a great treasure. A treasure—which we are told in another part of the Scripture—is worth more than jewels, gold, silver, and all the heart could know. There has been a search for this, not by the masses of men, but by what we might call superior men who are not satisfied to wallow in the mud.

I think of what Robert Browning said about certain men when he called them "finished and finite clods, untroubled by a spark."

These "finished and finite clods" are like Esau. The difference between Jacob and Esau was that Esau was a finished and finite clod. Esau's name meant red clay. In many ways, he was a finer person to be around than his brother Jacob. Jacob, however, had one thing Esau did not have. He was troubled by a spark.

What treasure is this which I have spoken of and repeated throughout this book? It is the treasure called *wisdom*. I want to look at wisdom down at the human level.

Humanly speaking, wisdom is like a vitamin. That is, it does not nourish a body in itself, but if not present, nothing will nourish the body. A vitamin will not nourish the body, but if the vitamin is not present, a person can eat a five-pound beefsteak and it will not nourish him. A vitamin will make everything else work, which is an illustration of wisdom.

Suppose, for illustration's sake, a man decided to become an artist and paint portraits. He invests $10,000 in the studio with pallets and brushes and easels and canvasses. A light coming through the window illuminates the whole room with the proper lighting. There was a tile floor, soft pastel walls, and other things to inspire him. He was equipped to be one of the greatest artists in the world.

Suppose also, models came to his studio, and against the window overlooking the scenery, were ravishing in their beauty. Yet that man could lack just one thing and never be able to paint one picture.

That lack would be sight. His sight would be the vitamin that makes everything else work. It would be that which gives meaning to everything else and without which leaves everything meaningless. The most beautiful model, the most marvelous scenery, the most expensive equipment would be worthless to a blind man.

Carry this illustration over into the area of wisdom. Such a thing as wisdom exists, but it is not the same as knowledge or education. It is not the same as intellect or talent. These things men have and are good, but they can have them for a lifetime and then must relinquish them. When their hand stretches out in the last gasp of death, they must give them up and they will not have gained them anything because they did not have wisdom.

A higher wisdom exists and embraces not only this world but also the life hereafter and forever, and that wisdom is with God. Down through the ages men have sought this wisdom. The Persians, the Egyptians, the Chinese, the Japanese, the Hindus—you find them everywhere, searching for this wisdom. I believe it is because man was made in the image of God, and it is the tattered fragments, the battered remnants of that image of God left in a fallen and lost soul that makes him salvageable, while he is still on the earth, and while it is still possible for God to get to him.

Human wisdom has given us poetry, art, and religions. The wisdom of God is all-embracing, the key to every door, the secret to all mysteries, but men cannot always find it. They may live a lifetime, die, and never find it. Socrates walked up and down Greece and taught his followers many wonderful truths, among them that no one could find true wisdom. He did not find it while he was alive, and some still say it is not to be found anywhere.

The book of Ecclesiastes is a treatise on the subject, a seeking after wisdom and not finding it and dying without it. This is not human learning. Anyone can learn if he has a decent mind, if he works at it enough, and that is true of most people. They buckle down to business, memorize, and they can learn almost anything.

But God's wisdom, the divine mystery, makes its possessor wiser than philosophers and learned men, wiser than scientists and geniuses. It gives him the secret of life and secures for him that which has been called the ultimate good and makes all things work for him. This is what the old Hebrew writers believed true wisdom was. It was a friend. It was a guide that would take you by the hand and lead you through the wilderness into the promised land. It would grow brighter day by day unto the perfect day, and it was this valuable mysterious gift of God that came to man.

"Where will we find it?" Job says.

> Surely there is a vein for the silver, and a place for gold where they fine it. Iron is taken out of the earth, and brass is molten out of the stone. He setteth an end to darkness, and searcheth out all perfection: the stones of darkness, and the shadow of death. The flood breaketh out from the inhabitant; even the waters forgotten of the foot: they are dried up, they are gone away from men. As for the earth, out of it cometh bread: and under it is turned up as it were fire. The stones of it are the place of sapphires: and it hath dust of gold.
>
> Job 28:1–6

One of the most beautiful passages in all of literature is this: "There is a path which no fowl knoweth, and which the vulture's eye hath not seen: The Lion's whelps have not trodden it, though the fierce lion passed by it" (Job 28:7–8).

This wisdom raises him to the level of angels, the fowls of the air. I have seen them floating for hours without moving a wing. Taking advantage of the air currents, tipping this way and that, gracefully circling and looking down, they are looking for food, and when they find something they want, they dive for it. But there is a path which no fowl knows, and which no vulture's eye has seen. The lion's whelps have not trodden it, though they have learned the jungle paths. Where shall wisdom be found and where is the place of understanding?

This wisdom cannot be purchased at any price.

> Man knoweth not the price thereof; neither is it found in the land of the living. The depth saith, It is not in me: and the sea saith, It is not with me. It cannot be gotten for gold, neither shall silver be weighed for the price thereof.
>
> Job 28:13–15

Nothing that comes from God can be purchased with money. It has no monetary value. The one thing God has to offer us and the only thing we absolutely need is His wisdom. Flowing from that wisdom is the solution to all the problems that we could ever face. To know the wisdom of God in its fullness is to experience life as God intended it to be.

We put a price tag on everything from a human standpoint, which is how our world works. We cannot, however, bring that over into our relationship with God. Our relationship with God must be based upon God's ways and not our ways. This wisdom that comes from on high, this divine breath that settles down upon us is what enables us to understand God and our relationship to Him.

To fear God, out of which flows wisdom, is to submit myself to God unconditionally and without any personal agenda. When I come to God as He invites me to come, I will have what God intends for me to have.

❦ ALL THAT I AM I OWE TO THEE ❦

Thy thoughts, O God, how manifold,
more precious unto me than gold!
I muse on their infinity,
awaking I am still with thee.

The Psalter, 1912

8

How to Access the Wisdom of God

O Holy Spirit, my wisdom fails so mightily, but when I look to Thee and allow that divine breath to fill my heart with divine wisdom, I begin to understand Thee and praise Thee forevermore. Let me not stay my heart till I have discovered Thee in all Thy fullness. Amen.

Man spends all his time and energy seeking that true wisdom which can only be found in God. The devil might know something about it, or about death and destruction, or hell or Hades. He might even know where it is. Death and destruction go hand-in-hand before their grinning skulls on top of the mausoleum, and say, "We're looking for wisdom."

The basis of this is because we have been made in the image of God and still have a tattered remnant of that image. We sense we are on our way to death and destruction, and we want to know how to get out of it.

"Can you tell us the way out?" But destruction and death say, "We have heard the fame thereof with our ears but that's all."

The dead man cannot come back to tell you, and hell cannot tell us, so we ask the question, "Where then shall wisdom be found?" That is the burning question in the heart of every person. In our own heart, we cannot find it. Then in Job 28:23 we read, "God understandeth the way thereof, and he knoweth the place thereof."

Man has a deep restlessness within him because he was created in the image of God and for God's purpose and pleasure. He was created to experience God in His fullness. The thing that has stopped this from happening is his relying upon man's wisdom, which consists of scholarship, business, inventions, psychology, and yes, even theology. No matter how successful a man is in these endeavors, there still remains a void within that can never be filled.

Why does he not remember this? Why does he not seek God?

With diligence, man can find just about anything, but he can never discover God on his own terms. Therefore, the gnawing question is why men do not think of God. He should be the first source a man turns to. If people knew God, their problems would be solved.

Some people make a business of trying to help people answer questions that can only be answered by God. Their counseling is based upon human wisdom, which can only go so far. They cannot cross the line and step over into divine wisdom.

I have often thought about why God is not always a priority in our life experiences. When we have a problem, why do we not go to God, who is the source of all wisdom? That should be our first thought. Instead, we tend to pursue man's wisdom. Do we think we can outsmart God?

It is a wonderful thing when you come to the conclusion that only God can help. Only God contains the wisdom that will lift you out of the problems you find yourself sinking into. This mystery, out of which all creation came, this vast golden womb out of which was born all the stars and galaxies, the worms that crawl, the winds that blow, things visible and invisible. Where is this found? It can only be found in God.

God raised his voice and said, "Behold, the fear of the Lord, that is wisdom; and to depart from evil is understanding" (Job 28:28).

The book of Job was written for the ages to come, telling us where we can find wisdom. Wisdom comes to the heart that is hungry for God. Wisdom is what God gives to the man who forsakes his sin and turns to his Savior.

Unfortunately, some people, including Christians, have come to the place where they expect a stunning angel with diamond-studded wings to come sweeping down and touch them on their forehead and say, "Be wise." That will never happen; it is not the way God works. God's gifts come to the simplehearted. This has always amazed me. God gives it to the babe. Babes and sucklings know more than the most knowledgeable man. God seems to hide these things from the wise and the prudent and reveals them to infants. God always teaches the humble His way and the meek He shows His judgment. Man always learns on his face, on his knees, and so the world turns its back. It will not humble itself.

God's wisdom flows from His heart into the heart of the man who has humbled himself before the Lord. God always insists that we turn from evil, repent, believe in God, and trust in the Lord. That is the beginning of wisdom.

We are more accustomed to dramas from Hollywood. However, God does not dramatize things like some ham actor reading from a script. God turns to the humble heart and says, "Here's my secret. Here's my jewel. Here is something more valuable than anything else in the universe: the soul of man. That is where I poured my likeness and my image. After man, I made angels and archangels and cherubim and seraphim and potentates and powers and dominions, and every name that is named. But it was not to angels or seraphim or cherubim that my Son was sent, but to man."

From God's standpoint, what is His jewel? From the Scriptures, we see that the heart of a man, the heart of a woman, the soul of a man or a woman is God's jewel. God whispers wisdom to the humble in heart. He whispers and pours out His secrets upon the person who hates sin, turns away from iniquity, and puts his trust in God his Savior. Do not forget that in the Old Testament men believed God was their Savior, just as we see in the New Testament. It was the same God.

In the Old Testament, they looked forward to His coming, and we look back on His coming, but it is the same Redeemer. Turning to God with reverential trust and holy obedience makes men wiser than the seven sages of eternity. This makes man more knowledgeable than if he had read and memorized all the encyclopedias of the world.

Now, you do not have to be young or smart. All you need to have is childlike faith. Oh, how happy is the person who finds this wisdom—this beautiful fear of Jehovah that results in departing from evil and turning to God and giving up all to Him in complete humility. However sinful, however reckless, however wild, however foolish our lives might have been in the past, we can turn it all over to God and receive from Him that flow of wisdom into our hearts.

Oh, what fools we have been. This is what the Bible means when it talks about a fool. It is a man who does not have wisdom. He has not had a visitation of God's wisdom on him. He may have knowledge, but he does not have wisdom. He may be very wise in the world's wisdom, but he does not have this visitation from on high, so the Bible calls him a fool.

A man had money enough and human wisdom enough, business acumen, as they say, and all the rest that he built his barns,

> And he said, This will I do: I will pull down my barns, and build greater; and there will I bestow all my fruits and my goods. And I will say to my soul, Soul, thou hast much goods laid up for many years; take thine ease, eat, drink, and be merry.
>
> Luke 12:18–19

That was man's evaluation, not God's.

> But God said unto him, thou fool, this night thy soul shall be required of thee: then whose shall those things be, which thou hast provided?
>
> Luke 12:20

He lived a lifetime and died without finding the wisdom that is at hand. In humility, bend your knees and look up. It is yours.

☙ Awake My Tongue, Thy Tribute Bring ❧

How vast His knowledge, how profound!
A deep where all our thoughts are drowned;
The stars He numbers, and their names
He gives to all those heavenly flames.

John Needham

9

The Manifestation
of God's Wisdom

Show me, O eternal Jehovah, Thy wisdom in all of its ramifications. Manifest Thy grace and wisdom in my life today as a witness to those around me. I surrender my heart and thoughts today to make way for Thine own wisdom in my life. Amen.

I have been reverently considering that infinite deep of ancient wisdom, and I think we know a little of what the psalmist meant when he said, "Deep calleth unto deep at the noise of thy waterspouts" (Psalm 42:7).

Let us take this a bit further and consider wisdom in its various forms. We will begin at the very lowest and then look at the eternal high wisdom in times of the tabernacle, which men call the natural law. We are adept at inventing phrases to dismiss God and get rid of Him, and so what the writers of the Old Testament called God, we call the laws of nature.

For example, when it rained, an Old Testament prophet said God was watering the hills from His chambers. But when it rains now, they simply call it precipitation. I would acknowledge that a man might say that and still be a good Christian, but the difference is very clear. To one, it was God, and to another, it is simply the condensation of water molecules because of a change in temperature. We sometimes put our scientific knowledge ahead of God. God is ruled out, and so it is with everything. Gravitation—God placed the stars in their courses. Now we know how to place moons in their courses.

Many look to God and hear a voice, saying, "Behold, God, wisdom is with God, and to humble yourself and pray and trust God and be righteous, that is wisdom."

The Old Testament book of Job is the wisdom book, and in the twelfth chapter, we find the other side of the picture altogether. It may sound contradictory, and if I were saying this, somebody would call me up or write me a letter and say, "You contradicted yourself." Job contradicts himself here (apparently, but not actually).

Let us be careful here of one thing. Let us never charge the writers of the Bible with mistakes or contradictions, because we will be red-faced in the day of judgment if we do so. God never makes mistakes and never contradicts himself, but He looks at two different sides of a thing, and reports what He sees, and it may sound as if He contradicts himself.

In the twelfth chapter of Job is wisdom in simple modification:

But ask now the beasts, and they shall teach thee; and the fowls of the air, and they shall tell thee: or speak to the earth, and it shall teach thee: and the fishes of the sea shall declare unto thee. Who knoweth not in all these the hand of the Lord has wrought this? In whose hand is the soul of every living thing, and the breath of all mankind. Doth not the ear try words? and the mouth taste his meat? With the ancient is wisdom; and in length of days understanding. With him is wisdom and strength, he hath counsel and understanding. Behold, he breaketh it down, and it cannot be built again: he shutteth up a man, and there can be no opening. Behold, he withholdeth the waters, and they dry up: also he sendeth them out, and they overturn the earth. With him is strength and wisdom: the deceived and the deceiver are his.

vv. 7–16

We are to remember this, that the deceived and the deceiver are His. God holds man in His hand, which does not mean that the deceived and the deceiver are His in the sense that they are His children. It only means He holds them in His hand and He will have His way at last.

Now, what do we get here? We get Job saying something like "I looked everywhere—from a coal mine to the death and destruction, and nobody could help me. I couldn't get wisdom." Then he says, ask the beast and they will teach you. What is he talking about here? He is talking about wisdom on another level, that which we call *instinct*. He is talking about how God in His infinite wisdom, behind the scenes, works things out.

The old apocryphal book says that God's wisdom is with God forever and He has poured her out upon all His works.

That is, wisdom that is being poured out upon the entire world.

What he is saying here is that there is a natural instinct. There is that in even the beast of the field. Even the creatures that fly around in the heavens above, walk around the earth, and swim in the sea. We call this natural law instinct. It is how birds fly away to the south in the fall and fly back in the spring toward the north. Why do Canada geese go into Canada, nest and have their young, and then take them south in the spring?

I will tell you this: They do not do it by any plans they have made. They do not have a king over them; they do not have anyone ruling them. They have not gone to school to learn how to do this. They have no engineers to figure it out for them. It is instinct put in them by the Creator.

Another type of wisdom is a secondary wisdom, possessed by man in varying degrees. We have men in high places: scientists, philosophers, statesmen, engineers, men who possess a measure of wisdom. But it is not the wisdom I have been talking about. It is more like common sense. It is thinned down, and belongs to fallen men. Everyone, even the gangster, the drunken man who staggers home, has sense enough to know where his home is, so God has given to everyone a modicum of this wonderful sense of things. But it does not save him. He must repent and be born again. But, nonetheless, he has a gift from God to him.

I know some people are afraid to say that a man has wisdom, because the Bible warns a man about that. They are afraid to say a man can be righteous because the Bible says man does not have righteousness in himself. The critic might say the Bible is contradictory. But instead of using words properly, they are a slave to words.

There is such a thing as the absolute and the relative. There is such a thing as that which cannot be improved upon, which God has, and then there is that which can be improved upon, which man has.

The man who invented the electric light was a wise man, but his wisdom was relative. The great God, who made him, has absolute, unlimited, infinite wisdom. When the Bible says there is none good but God, it means there is none absolutely good, as God is. When it says there was a good man, full of the Holy Ghost, it means the man was relatively good.

We have allowed words to confuse us, and we have not the patience to be reasonable about them. If a man says, "I want to be holy," someone will rush in and say, "You can't be holy. Don't you know only God is holy?" If he says, "I prayed to God that I might be righteous," they say, "You can't be righteous. Don't you know only God is righteous?" The thing is we take on God's holiness and righteousness when we are born again and He lives in and through us.

God has said, "Be ye holy; for I am holy" (1 Peter 1:16). He did not say be suddenly as holy as I am, but the Holy Spirit makes you holy as He is allowed to dwell in you.

God makes the rain to fall on the just and the unjust. He waters the earth for all, even for the hardest sinner in all the world. We all depend upon God to water the earth. He sends the sunshine and melts the snow and warms the earth, and grass begins to grow and fruit begins to appear, and the hardest sinner is just as dependent upon God as the saint who prays and fasts and works. So God gives a certain degree of wisdom to all.

🙰 AWAKE, MY TONGUE, THY TRIBUTE BRING 🙰

Through each bright world above, behold
Ten thousand thousand charms unfold;
Earth, air, and mighty seas combine
To speak His wisdom all divine.

John Needham

10

God's Wisdom Is Poured Out on His Creation

O Lord God, Thy wisdom has been poured into my heart, creating such a longing for Thee that nothing in this world can satisfy. Fill my heart to overflowing with thyself, in Jesus' name. Amen.

In continuing to look at God's creation, we see the effect of His wisdom on that creation. God has filled the valley with manna, but we do not have any receptacles to take it in.

The word *receptacle* and the word *receptivity* are allies. Receptacle here is that which is receptive; it holds things, and God has poured His wisdom upon mankind, just as He has poured His sunshine upon mankind.

Imagine certain creatures that live in the dark caverns of the earth that have never seen the sun. They have a certain amount of wisdom within the confines of their environment, but there is a higher degree of wisdom.

We have been talking about that eternal wisdom that came down to the lowest tabernacles, dwelling in the breast of a dove or a duck or a goose or a worm that crawls away, hides, and wraps itself in a cocoon awaiting the warm spring. Then there is the wisdom that God has given to mankind, and he is able to receive it. Wise men there are; presidents must be wise men, and so with prime ministers, governors, and mayors of cities. They must have a certain degree of wisdom, but it is a relative thing.

There is a higher degree of wisdom than this. That is what I am referring to here. The infusion of eternal wisdom, the opening of the inward eyes, that further enlightenment, anointed sight. Bible teachers today should spend more time waiting on God, fasting, praying, and asking Him for open eyes and anointed hearts than they do writing articles about mysticism and what doesn't belong in the Bible.

We sing about it in our hymns—Baptists, Presbyterians, Quakers, Methodists, and Lutherans, going back as far as the Middle Ages.

This effusion of superior wisdom is a gift imparted by God in addition to the gift of wisdom that He gives the birds so they know to fly south and that which He gives man to invent a spaceship or an electric light. This effusion of superior wisdom is something you either have or you don't. It does not come gradually to anyone. So a man is either born or he is not. He is either born again or he has not been born again; he cannot come into that gradually. The doctrine of gradualness is from the devil to keep the church of Christ from going forward.

Some are saying that being truly born again is an ideal, but you never can attain it. If any prophet, apostle, or anyone else would come to me and say, "I demand that you seek, but I promise you you'll never find. I demand that you travel, but I tell you, you will never reach your destination. I demand that you aspire, but you will never reach your aspirations"—I would say to that one, "Go back to your meditations. I will go out, get all I can out of the world and have myself a good time. For tomorrow I die." If all that we've been teaching is a misty idea that can never be reached, I do not want to be bothered with it.

I do believe, however, that it is not an ideal that cannot be reached. I believe that God has promised His people an outpouring of Holy Spirit baptisms and effusions of power and wisdom and grace.

There is another kind of wisdom, and that is a wisdom that for want of a better word, I will call a *divine migratory instinct*. "No man can come to me," John the beloved writes, "except the Father which hath sent me draw him: and I will raise him up at the last day" (John 6:44).

There is a light that lighteth every man that cometh into the world. It is a kind of a divine migratory instinct that turns our steps toward God.

God distributes the migratory instinct as He will. He gives the thought to a man that says, *This is not my home.* Jacob had it; Esau did not. Of the two, Jacob had this instinct. One night out on the desert, in the howling wilderness, he saw a ladder rising up from the earth. Something in his heart cried out to God, and Jacob was converted.

That which David had, Saul did not. Saul was more handsome than David. David had a ruddy complexion and was small; Saul was a great strapping fellow. They would depict him as a basketball player today because he was head and shoulders above everybody else. He was a fine-looking fellow, but he never indicated that he heard the voice. David heard it. David could sin, but he also could repent. It doesn't matter that you have been a great sinner if you can repent.

A man who is willing to repent will find God.

Of the two apostles Peter and Judas, one denied Christ and one betrayed Him. Both spent three years with Jesus, watched Him heal the sick, raise the dead, still the waves, turn water into wine, make the blind to see, and the deaf to hear. Both had the same opportunity. Peter got scared and ran like a coward, but later he wept because he knew he had sinned. He had that instinct from God; Judas did not. So although Judas was an apostle, he died and went to his own place.

Our problem today is that we are engrossed with *things*. We are pursuing things instead of pursuing God. We are running after things instead of running after God. "Man of God, flee these things; and follow after righteousness," said Timothy (1 Timothy 6:11). But we are not fleeing, and what light we have, we have ignored.

There is "the true Light, which lighteth every man that cometh into the world" (John 1:9) so that he is without excuse. But many have ignored that nudge and not sought the light of the gospel. Others have trampled it under their feet, turning their backs on it.

We cannot understand all the profundities of theology. I confess that I do not understand everything in the Bible. In Matthew, it says, "Come unto me, all ye that labour and are heavy laden, and I will give you rest" (11:28). What does that mean exactly? But if you have a feeling that God has spoken to you or is speaking to you now, you had better do something about it immediately.

Thank God on your knees that He did not pass you up, but has allowed the light to flash upon your spirit and tell you to come home. And if you have a migratory feeling within you and you know this is not your home, this world is no place for you, repent and turn away from sin and believe on the Lord Jesus Christ as your Savior.

For wisdom dwells with God and He pours her out upon all His works in the degree they are able to absorb it, and the wisest man is the one who turns to the Lord in repentance and faith. There is no greater proof of wisdom than that of turning to the Lord and seeking righteousness through Jesus Christ.

O BOUNDLESS WISDOM, GOD MOST HIGH

O boundless Wisdom, God most high,
O Maker of the earth and sky,
Who bid'st the parted waters flow
In heaven above, on earth below.
Author unknown, trans. from
Latin by Gabriel Gillett

11

The Benefits
of Eternal Wisdom

*Heavenly Father, open my eyes to recognize Thy hand
in my life. I praise Thee for the enrichment that has
come into my life as I have embraced Thy wisdom.
May I be aware of my surroundings in light of what
Thou art doing. Amen.*

In the book of Proverbs, you will discover eloquent but
urgent exhortations to seek wisdom—to labor for it, to
sell everything to get it, to get it by all means. In chapter
4, the Holy Spirit urges the wandering sons of men to "receive my sayings; and the years of thy life shall be many" (v.
10). Elsewhere in the Old Testament, in the Psalms and in
the books of the prophets, wisdom is presented in equally

poetic and colorful terms, whereas the language in the New Testament is more doctrinal.

One question I pose is simply this: What does this offer us? If this is merely rhetoric, of what value is it? How does this change my life today?

The Scriptures speak often about the wise man and the fool. The wise man has been illuminated with a divine infusion of wisdom from the heart of God. The fool has not. In the Scriptures, a fool cannot distinguish the chaff from the wheat. He does not know a pearl from a grain of corn; he does not know a diamond from glass; he does not know the living from the dead. He completely lacks the ability to distinguish the lasting value of things.

Human society is built on the errors of fools. This sounds brutal, but in the context of the Scriptures it is very kind. I say this because a fool acts without regard to future consequences—as though there were not another world besides this one and he was not intending to die. The strange thing is, he lives this way only in his moral life. Intellectually, he knows he's not going to be here always, and he makes sure his insurance is in place and writes a will and arranges for his family after he is gone. However, morally he lives as if he were going to be here forever, as if there were no death and no future life.

That is what a fool is, and again, a philosophy upon which our whole society is built.

Take ambition, for instance. Ambition drives men, enslaves them, and then at last hurls its victims down in disappointment. Human society has also arranged amusements in order to quiet the victim while death creeps nearer all the time.

Scripture says wisdom cures this. "If thou criest after knowledge, and liftest up thy voice for understanding . . .

then shalt thou understand the fear of the Lord, and find the knowledge of God" (Proverbs 2:3, 5). There comes an illumination to the heart that enables you to understand the fear of the Lord and find the knowledge of God. Again, in Proverbs 2:9, it says, "Then shalt thou understand righteousness, and judgment, and equity; yea, every good path."

Is it true, then, that the average man on the street lacks understanding of righteousness, judgment, equity, and every good path? Look at the many who are seeking direction for their lives. The trouble is, a great deal of this seeking is simply a desire to have a guide that will help him get what he wants, get all the fun he can out of life and not have to pay the consequences. Many counselors today are doing that very thing. They meet with young people, instructing them in a manner that will enable them to have their own way, miss the cross, miss the dying to self, miss repentance, and ultimately miss the will of God. But the wisdom of God imparts discernment that will save you from the wrong choice and the false counselor.

Divine wisdom can also save us from worthless pursuits—those that are not God's will for us.

It is better for Christians to sit on their hands until the judgment than to undertake pursuits God has not willed for them. It is the wisdom of God that enables a man to be delivered from these pursuits, giving him discernment so that he will know God's truth and be delivered from false doctrine.

Too many people are led away by the suspicious, smooth, empty sophistry of false doctrines, and it takes the Holy Spirit to teach us the difference. We should not only memorize the Word, which is an excellent thing to do, but also know the difference between truth and error in applying the Word faithfully.

No one upon whom the holy light of wisdom has shone would ever follow a false god. The voices of false shepherds are heard everywhere. If you try to meet a false shepherd on his own terms, he will win because he has been taught to respond to that. The true believer hears the voice of God and knows His voice.

Moreover, wisdom enables us to recognize God's hand. Many cannot see it, or they mistake the hand of man for God's. In the Old Testament, I find this statement in various forms over and over again: "And ye shall know that I am Jehovah." God wants to reveal himself to His people.

Often we do not recognize the hand of God leading us providentially. The church fathers preached on the providence of God. They said, God "plays" the world as a man plays checkers, and every move He makes works with everything else to accomplish His will. He moves down the paths of the universe, making all things fit together—playing the pieces around the board so as to win for you. You may not immediately see the providence of God, but the Holy Ghost will help you so that you are able to look up and say, "Thank you, God, I see now Thy hand in all of this."

The wisdom of God also enables us to recognize His presence.

In the Old Testament, we read how Jacob was awakened suddenly from a sound asleep. I imagine him leaping to his feet and looking about him before declaring, "Surely the Lord is in this place; and I knew it not. And he was afraid, and said, How dreadful is this place! this is none other but the house of God, and this is the gate of heaven" (Genesis 28:16–17).

Oh, what a different world it would be, what a different life we would live, what a different service we would render, and what a different death we would die if we were able to see the presence of God in all things all of the time.

In prayer meetings, I often hear people pray, "Thou hast said that Thou wouldst be with us; therefore, Thou art with us." Logic. Jacob was a logician enough to know God was everywhere. But the reality never hit his heart until that providential night: *Why, God is in this place, and I just now am waking up to it.* What a world this would be, with all its sin and crime and all the rest, if we had that light of recognition to know the presence of God with us at all times.

The wisdom of God also enables us to know God's chastisement.

When trouble comes, it may be one of two things. It may be the price you are paying for how you have lived. Or, it may be your heavenly Father disciplining you to make you a better person. If you have not the light of God, you will rely on your sense of logic and think it is the devil causing the trouble, or you will blame it on somebody else. Without illumination, you will not know if God is disciplining you.

Some of God's dear people go through life with clenched fists. They pray, read their Bible, attend church, give to missions, but they are tense and struggling, thinking, *Nobody is going to put anything over on me.* I suppose not, but how wonderful it would be if we could only see the hand of God in everything and not have to struggle. Paul tells us that we do not war against flesh and blood. You never have to fight people if you get a spiritual viewpoint enabling you to see what God is trying to do in certain situations. If board members, deacons, elders, and all the children of God could have a divine illumination, it would enable them to think like God, and there would be little reason for fusses and divisions and quarrels in the churches.

But we tend to do things in the way of the world. We try to reason things out the way they do at First National Bank or General Motors, and put it down on a business basis to reason it out by logic. We do have problems in the churches, and it is because we do not seek God's hand. We do not know what God is trying to do, and we do not see as God sees.

If you know that God is chastening you as you would chasten a loving son, it would take the bitterness out of it. You could even smile through your tears. You could be glad even when things are going against you if you knew that God was in it.

But you may not know it, because every time God raises a hand to chasten you, the devil tells you that you are getting your just punishment. God allows someone to work on you and persecute you, and the devil will say, "You're no good" or "That person is treating you wrongly. That's unjust."

I always cringe when I hear the word *unfair*. Nobody ever heard a holy man use the word, because the Christian does not know anything about fairness. He does not live in a world where people treat him fairly. The world did not treat Christ fairly. Who treated the apostles justly? No one. God's people do not fight back. When we are accused, we do not accuse again. When they pour coals of fire on us, we do not get angry. We try by kindness to pour a different kind of fire on their heads.

This is the problem with the church of Christ today. We do not live in this area, this glorious plateau where we recognize the hand of God, where we are conscious of the presence of

God, see the chastisement of God, and see the truth of God. But God says, "Happy is the man that findeth wisdom, and the man that getteth understanding" (Proverbs 3:13). "Wisdom is the principal thing; therefore get wisdom: and with all thy getting get understanding" (Proverbs 4:7).

O BOUNDLESS WISDOM, GOD MOST HIGH

E'en so on us who seek Thy face
Pour forth the waters of Thy grace;
Renew the fount of life within,
And quench the wasting fires of sin.
Author unknown, trans. from
Latin by Gabriel Gillett

12

Divine Wisdom Illuminates
the Face of Christ

*O Eternal Wisdom from on high, follow me, search me,
and lead me in the way everlasting. Let me penetrate
the cloud of unknowing and see Thy face and allow it
to transform every aspect of my being. My heart longs
to see Thee in the beauty of Thy holiness. Never let me
wander from Thy presence, O Lord. Amen.*

Perhaps the most important aspect of divine wisdom is
the illumination of the face of Christ. Life moves on,
rising up and down, until you are always waiting for
a period and never finding one. "For God," the apostle Paul
said, "who commanded the light to shine out of darkness,
hath shined in our hearts, to give the light of the knowledge

of the glory of God in the face of Jesus Christ" (2 Corinthians 4:6).

It is the face of Jesus Christ that is my focus here. To know Him other than by hearsay is the great goal of the Christian experience. A person can know someone superficially, but when you begin to stare into their face you begin to see them in their reality.

When I look into the face of Jesus Christ, I begin to see the reality of God. This is not just religion. This is not just something to do as my conscience dictates. This is the reality of knowing God in the most intimate fashion possible.

Looking into someone's face is how we can judge whether they are lying or telling the truth. There are people who call themselves "face readers" and somehow make quite a good living at it. I'm not suggesting that here. What I am suggesting is that there is a level of knowing God that is face-to-face, and in that experience we see the glory of God.

There once lived a great man by the name of Henry Suso. I have read his writings and have tried to sing his hymns. I do not know their tune, so I make them up as I go along, or try to remember one and make it fit. However, Henry Suso has written some great hymns and some great devotional writings. He said this about himself: "In my earlier youth, a very impetuous soul, I strayed to the path of error."

In his spiritual imagining, he saw Eternal Wisdom approaching him, met him, and led him through both rough and smooth ways until he was brought back to God again and to the ways of truth. He spoke to wisdom as to the Lord, and said, "O beloved, gentle Lord, since the days of my childhood, my heart has sought for something with an ardent thirst, and Lord, what it is I cannot tell and I do not fully understand."

Then the voice of wisdom spoke, "It is I, Eternal Wisdom, who hath chosen thee from all eternity with the embrace of my eternal providence. I have supported thee in the way. . . . Before you were converted, no matter how much you enjoyed yourself, there was always an emptiness and bitterness. . . . At first, you experienced the excitement of remembering the fun of an evening. Slowly that faded and the hollow feelings began to come back into your heart. . . . You have been searching and searching, but that was not what you sought."

Some people have this thirst and some do not. I don't know how to explain it. Some are satisfied, enjoy the world and its pleasures, and it leaves no bitterness when it is over. I suppose we could chisel into their gravestones: "Ichabod, the glory has departed. Let him alone, he is joined to his idols. Don't pray for him." But there are others who are miserable, and fun cannot help them for long. Amusement cannot help them. Entertainment does not satisfy.

They say, "O blessed, divine Lord, I have looked everywhere and I can't find what I want." The Lord says there is a reason for that: "I've been providentially working in you and you didn't know it. I have been working within you my providential guidance, part of my plan from eternity for you. I have turned your sweetness into bitterness and your happiness to sadness. I've turned your fullness to emptiness as I have sought you."

How wonderful it is to know that God is after you.

Francis Thompson wrote a poem called "The Hound of Heaven." I don't like its title. I cannot bring myself even in a title to allow a figure of speech calling God the Hound of Heaven, but nevertheless, the poem tells about how he fled God down through the years. It is a brilliant thing, telling how he ran from God, fleeing from God, yet always God followed him and found him.

I am not an emotional man, but I can easily get emotional over that picture.

God says, "I've been following you, son. It was I who was with you when you took your long walks as a boy on Sunday afternoons. Your long walks up the path and down the railroad tracks and out into the woods, enjoying nature, then came back and went to bed miserable."

Again, Suso says, "I enrolled in this and that, and did all those crazy things. I thought it was the thing to do. I was seventeen, and thought I ought to be out having myself a whale of a time. So I was out doing those things, but I always came back miserable. Always when I would go to bed at night, I would think, *What's the use?* So I quit the whole business and gave it all up—I strayed from the path of error."

What was it? Suso says, "It was eternal wisdom that had chosen me . . . with the embrace of eternal providence, and supported me so often in the way. If I would know Him in His uncreated divinity, I would learn to know Him in His suffering humanity.

"That is the way to eternal bliss. God knows me at my best, and He knows me in my suffering humanity." He knows because He is the suffering Savior. Let us put Him as the focus of our attention and in faith and let us press close to His heart. Thomas Aquinas said, "If thou lackest strength to take high flights to spirituality, then hide thee in the wounds of Jesus."

You cannot take high flights, but you can hide in the wounds of Jesus, and if you know what the voice of eternal wisdom is, you are hearing it. Even now, you can go to Jesus

Christ, who gave himself for you and there in His suffering humanity took all your sins on himself and died. This is wonderful news!

❦ O LORD, THY ALL DISCERNING EYES ❦

O Lord, Thy all discerning eyes
My inmost purpose see;
My deeds, my words, my thoughts, arise
Alike disclosed to Thee:
My sitting down, my rising up,
Broad noon, and deepest night,
My path, my pillow, and my cup,
Are open to Thy sight.

John Q. Adams

13

The Pursuit
of Excellent Wisdom

*O God, my soul cries out to Thee in desperation. Help
me to overcome the weakness of my own soul and trust
in Thy wisdom alone. I praise Thee for Thy faithfulness
in pursuing me and going to the ultimate end to rescue
me from myself. Amen.*

Today we hear the voice of what our fathers called
excellent wisdom, and they dedicated themselves
to the pursuit of it.

We hear this wisdom crying to the sons of men, and
strangely enough, not where you would expect her voice to
be raised.

Wisdom crieth without; she uttereth her voice in the streets:
She crieth in the chief place of concourse, in the openings

of the gates: in the city she uttereth her words, saying, How long, ye simple ones, will ye love simplicity? and the scorners delight in their scorning, and fools hate knowledge? Turn you at my reproof: behold, I will pour out my spirit unto you, I will make known my words unto you.

Proverbs 1:20–23

Not in the house of worship, not in the theological seminary or the schools, but she cries without. She utters her voice in the streets and cries in the chief place of concourse, and at the opening of these gates in Old Testament times where the authority was, sitting inside the gates.

The voice of this excellent wisdom is crying to the sons of men, not only in the churches, but in the conscience, and in the funeral train as it goes by. Everywhere this eternal wisdom is calling, and in her calling she is dividing people into three classes: the simple ones, the scorners, and the fools.

This is the Holy Spirit, the voice of excellent wisdom. And these three classes are in such desperate need of the help of wisdom. I am going to turn these around and look at them not in the order in which they occur here, but in the order that will be easier for us to handle.

I have given this some long and very careful consideration. I have looked into the original language and the commentaries and searched until what I say will not be merely a man's guess, but it will be the winnowed wisdom of the Scriptures and of better minds who have expounded the Scriptures. In my definition of the three classes—the simple ones, the scorners, and the fools—you will notice this wisdom cries without and she says, "How long, ye simple ones" and "How long, ye scorners" and "How long, ye fools."

1. The Scorners

First, think about the scorners. The scorner scoffs at the voice of wisdom. I think it is not too much to say that of the three classes, the scorner is the worst. He does not necessarily reject all religion. It is not that he is not a religious person, but he holds himself above the advice of others, considers himself clever, and smiles at all those enthusiasts. We read in the Psalms, "Blessed is the man that walketh not in the counsel of the ungodly, nor standeth in the way of sinners, nor sitteth in the seat of the scornful" (1:1).

Personally, I have always been afraid of souring down and hardening up into a self-assured, clever man who has seen all kinds of religion. I know just where to put it, classify it, and what to do with every flash of fire that I see and every gust of heavenly wind, and every shining countenance. I have always been afraid that I would get into that place and find myself, unknown to me, sitting in the seat of the scornful. The voice of wisdom cries out to the scorner.

He has not much of a chance, but he does have a chance. He can come back, even though he has gotten himself into that state of mind.

2. The Fools

Then we come to the fools. How long, wisdom says, will fools love to continue to be fools? "Ye fools, how long will you hate knowledge?"

Remembering the words of Jesus, that a man should not call his brother a fool—and would be in grave danger of judgment if he did—and also conscious of my own acts of folly, I speak in great charity here and as a friend of excellent wisdom. The Bible has a great deal to say about fools and foolishness and folly, and they all come, of course, from the same stem. The Bible speaks, as far as I know, only of moral fools. Have you noticed that in the Scripture there is practically nothing at all said about insanity? I can only think of one instance. David, in order to get out of a tight spot, had been brought before the king and he made a face and began to slobber on his beard. They said, "Well, you brought a mad man; take him out of here." So David escaped by pretending. David was probably the first one to plead insanity before the court and got away with it. The Bible has very little to say about subnormal people or people with weak minds, but it has a great deal to say about fools, because a fool may be brilliant, maybe even be a genius. A fool may have an amazingly high IQ and yet be a moral fool. According to Scripture, a moral fool is someone who is spiritually dull.

Isaiah spoke of this in Isaiah 6:9–10:

> And he said, Go, and tell this people, Hear ye indeed, but understand not; and see ye indeed, but perceive not. Make the heart of this people fat, and make their ears heavy, and shut their eyes; lest they see with their eyes, and hear with their ears, and understand with their heart, and convert, and be healed.

This is a judgment of God—a judicial judgment of a sovereign God upon people who have played with truth. They became fools. They were unable to grasp spiritual things, and Paul delineates the frightening progress downward of the nations in First Corinthians, chapter 1.

Again, what the Bible means by a fool is not a man with a low IQ. The Bible speaks only in great kindness of sick people or anyone who might be classified as subnormal or abnormal. But this is a moral thing, and when the voice of excellent wisdom sounds in the marketplaces, where politicians assemble and where men buy and sell on the street corners, the voice of wisdom cries out, and she is talking to fools, among others.

How do we recognize the fool? The wisdom books of the Old Testament are full of examples of foolishness, but in Proverbs 12:15, it tells us that "the way of a fool is right in his own eyes," which is one of the marks of the fool.

The humility and meekness that even our own ignorance ought to bring us, a fool never thinks about. Morally, he is always right in his own eyes. Proverbs 14:16 says, "The fool rageth, and is confident." We might describe him as an egotistical extrovert with a savage temper. He rages and is confident. The moral fool is always sure of himself, and if you try to squeak in your testimony as meekly and kindly as you may, he nevertheless will rage and be confident in himself, because he is always right in his own eyes.

In the Old Testament, Job's wife was an excellent example of this. When Job got sick with boils from head to toe, and was lying on an ash heap, scraping himself with a pottery fragment, Job's wife said to him, "Curse God, and die" (Job 2:9). He replied to her, "Thou speakest as one of the foolish women speaketh." He did not call her crazy, but said in effect, "You don't sound like a believer. You sound like a fool." In other words, her attitude toward God and her wholly irreverent attitude toward life indicated that she was a foolish woman, and Job did not hesitate to say that she was. That is the last time we hear of her.

Another example is found in the New Testament at the close of the Sermon on the Mount, where Jesus compares the one who hears the Word and does it to a wise man who builds his house on a rock, and the one who hears but does not do what he knows to be right to the foolish man who builds his house on sand (Matthew 7:24–26).

Anybody knows that if you build a house on sand, the house is going to go down the first time there comes a gully washer of a rain. Yet the person Jesus refers to here, though he might have in every other way been intelligent, could not see ahead morally. He could not forecast his own future and place himself in a position where he was able to judge the result of his own actions. Jesus called him a foolish man.

It is like a moral foresight. The foolish man lives as if he will not live again, as if this were the only world there is, and if you said to him, "Mr. Jones, do you believe there is an afterlife?" He would say, "Certainly. I'm not an atheist. I go to church once a Sunday." And if you said to him, "Do you believe you're going to live again?" He would say, "Certainly. I believe in the resurrection from the dead."

The point is, though he believes those things, he lives as if they were not so. The man who lives as if the truth were not true is as bad as the man who denies the truth. God judges a man by how he lives the truth, not by how he parrots the truth. So there are two outstanding examples of a fool.

3. The Simple Ones

The simple ones are the uncommitted ones. They are neither on God's side, nor are they particularly on the side of evil. They are a bit innocent yet. They are not scorners; they are not opinionated and stubborn and self-willed, but consciously ignorant. An ignorant man who is consciously ignorant may be a wise man before very long, or at least a learned man, but an ignorant man who does not know his ignorance, that is the scorner and the fool.

One of the biggest mistakes we make is to look out on what seems to be a happy world, or listen to music, and hear something going on at a nightclub, for instance, and think, *They must be a happy crowd.* But wait until they bid good-bye to the last one with whom they have had fun, and get home, and they are not happy at all.

Francis Bacon once said about a king, "It is indeed a terrible state to be in to be like a king: to have nothing to desire and nothing to fear." That is an awful state. The king can get anything he wants, just demand it and he can have it, so he has nothing to want, but everything to fear. That is your fool, your simple one, and your scorner, but they think they are happy. They are simply scared stiff, and a great deal of what we think is happiness is simply nervous whistling, walking past a graveyard. People are simply frightened and may even be sick of themselves.

It is a wonderful moment in the life of any man when he becomes sick and weary of himself. As long as you like to take a quick glance at yourself in the mirror, as long as you like to test yourself to see how wise you are, and otherwise measure yourself against someone else and come out ahead, there's not much hope, but when you get sick of yourself, then you may yet be simple.

The simple one is occasionally penitent. Have you ever seen people with waves of penitence? That is the description of a simple person. He is uncommitted, yet he is somewhat open-minded. He is open to influencing counsel. This simplicity, though, is not going to last long. "How long you simple ones, will you love simplicity?" The simple soul is salvageable. I do not say the scorner is not, because God follows scorners. I do not say the fool is not; I believe that all of us have had acts of folly and would classify as a fool for a time. And if the fool had no hope, why does God address him? Why does He say, "How long . . . will you . . . hate knowledge? Turn you at my reproof." No, there is hope, even for the fool, and there is hope for the scorner, but there is a great deal more hope for the simple person.

I like simplehearted people. I like to see brilliant people sometimes, but they are hard to live around. You always feel inferior. I like the simplehearted, and I believe Jesus loved them. I like what Jesus said in Matthew 11:25: "I thank thee, O Father, Lord of heaven and earth, because thou hast hid these things from the wise and prudent, and hast revealed them unto babes."

The voice of excellent wisdom cries even to the fool and to the scorner, and says, "Turn at my reproof . . . I will pour out my spirit unto you, I will make known my words unto you" (Proverbs 1:23). These are the words of God to all kinds of people. For, you see, the fool and the scorner have to become simplehearted before they can be blessed, but they can only become simplehearted by humility and penitence.

☙ THINE, LORD, IS WISDOM, THINE ALONE ☙

Thine, Lord, is wisdom, Thine alone;
Justice and truth before Thee stand:
Yet, nearer to Thy sacred throne,
Mercy withholds Thy lifted hand.

> Ernst Lange

14

The Focus
of Excellent Wisdom

*Dear Lord Jesus, Thou alone who art Christ, honor my
repentance with forgiveness and a heart in tune with
Thee. Let me not flounder in the sea of my ignorance,
but rescue me and bring me to the shore of Thy heart.
Amen.*

I
t is quite interesting to see how this voice of wisdom falls
upon people and how it affects their life.

Gerhard Tersteegen, a preacher in the eighteenth century, was a man who would stand head and shoulders above
anyone for intelligence and culture, though he was a silk
weaver. He stood high, but he had a simplicity about him.
You also found it in the Wesleys—the Oxford men who
passed through the state of self-conscious learning and got

simplehearted. You also found simplicity in a man like Francis of Assisi and to a lesser degree in Martin Luther. I believe you will find it in almost all of the great saints, great souls, and great reformers.

They were persons who had put aside their foolishness, repented of their scornfulness, and allowed the Holy Ghost to chasten them until they were simplehearted. No man has ever committed sins enough that if he would humble his heart, become innocent like a child, and talk to God without trying to appear to be someone, God would not bless him. Nobody ever went down deep enough, was ever fool enough, ever sarcastically scornful enough about religion, that if he would repent, humble himself before God, God would not accept him as a little child. How wonderful this is to know.

If God were only addressing His message to nuclear scientists, perhaps a hundred of the leading minds of the nation, what would the rest of us do? I do not know anything about nuclear science. I just know the jargon I hear over the radio. I have read a few books, but I am no expert. If I had to stand up and say, "I'm going to teach you all about nuclear fission, and if you know that, you will be saved," how terrible that would be.

However, I can go to any one of these hundred leading minds of America and say, "I don't know a thing about your science, but I can tell you this, if you humble yourself like a little child, you can know my Savior." They can come down even if I cannot go up. That is the wisdom of salvation. Anybody can come down. A man on top of a mountain can come down. Just let yourself go, and you will come down, but not necessarily go up. So the Lord is not asking people to go up, just asking them to come down, even the scorner and the fool.

But humility and penance and sorrow of heart, just as a bee, as the poet said, soars for a bloom high as the highest peaks in England. Wherever there is bloom, there are bees, and whenever there is sorrow of heart, wherever there is grief of spirit, wherever there is inward sickness, there is the Holy Spirit.

That great Danish preacher Søren Kierkegaard talked about this terrible sickness unto death. Not every man can be a genius and be learned, but every learned genius can have the sickness unto death, and wherever you find that sickness unto death within the heart of a man, you will find the Holy Spirit. Excellent wisdom is there, hovering around like a dove of Noah's ark, and you can hear the whirl of holy wings.

There is not much hope for the scorner and the fool, but there is every hope for the simple one. You do not think you amount to much if you are just humble and common. But you are ready to turn just as you are, without one plea, to the cross of Jesus Christ. There is hope for you. "Turn you at my reproof: behold, I will pour out my spirit unto you, I will make known my words unto you" (Proverbs 1:23). What words? Words of forgiveness, words of cleansing, words of assurance, words of peace, words of confidence, and words of certainty. God says He will make known His words if we will turn at His reproof, giving every good hope for the simple person, that person who has not yet gone clear over and committed himself.

Hear that voice crying in the marketplace, crying on the buses and the elevated trains and at the concourse of the way:

How long will you go on in your foolishness? (see Proverbs 1:22).

Uncommitted persons are always in danger. Are *you* committed, and if so, to whom or to what? Now would be a wonderful moment to change, and commit yourself to God. Oh, how God wants committed people to stand before Him, to kneel before Him, in the public assembly or in the secret chamber. To commit themselves as one who swears allegiance to another country. Who raises his right hand before the authorities, and says, "I repudiate the King or the Queen, or whoever it is, and swear allegiance to the United States of America; I promise to take up arms in her defense, to obey her laws, respect her Constitution . . ." and then walk out a committed American citizen.

I pray that God will burden your heart to the point of moving forward in this area of commitment. If you remain simple and uncommitted, the devil can stampede you and force you into a place of commitment to the wrong side. Then it would be better for you had you never been born, than to have the light of judgment shine on your responsible head when it is too late.

I am not a visionary man, and I do not hear voices. Yet the Bible has so completely sold me on the idea that there is a voice in every gale, that there is "the sound of a going in the tops of the mulberry trees" (2 Samuel 5:24). And the voice sounding through God's universe is saying, "Turn ye, turn ye, turn ye to me at my reproof. Turn ye all. Why will you die? Turn to me, simple ones. Come unto me, all ye that labor and are heavy laden, and I will give you rest." I hear it, and I worship and thank God that I hear it. Do you hear it? Do you hear Him say, "Turn ye unto me all ye

116

foolish ones, all ye simple ones, all ye uncommitted ones, turn ye unto me"?

THY WAYS, O LORD, WITH WISE DESIGN

My favored soul shall meekly learn
To lay her reason at Thy throne;
Too weak Thy secrets to discern,
I'll trust Thee for my guide alone.

Ambrose Serle

15

The Practicality
of God's Wisdom

My heart, O God, needs Thy most sacred protection.
Keep me from the infiltration of sin into my life so that
I may glorify Thee in everything I do. Do not, O Lord,
let me be caught up in my own wisdom, but rather to
render completely to Thee. May my fellowship honor
Thee in every regard. Amen.

In my opinion, we have done this generation of Christians a great disservice. There has been too much religious education, too much study of methodology, too much effort to know how to reach young minds by tricks, and not enough confidence in the Holy Ghost and the Word of God.

We have given to this generation the impression that there is a place or state that you can enter by accepting Christ, where you can lower your guard, for the fight is over, the battle is won, and all because of what Christ did. You have nothing to do. I would like to say to you—and I would be a liar if I said anything else, and you would hate me for it: The Pilgrim Way is a perilous way.

You are born into the world, you are born in sin, you are here, and it is up to you to get out of sin and out of this world to heaven above. However, let me tell you, there is no easy way. It is a false teaching to say otherwise: "My son, if sinners entice thee, consent thou not. If they say, Come with us, let us lay wait for blood, let us lurk privily for the innocent without cause. . . . My son, walk not thou in the way with them; refrain thy foot from their path" (Proverbs 1:10–11, 15).

Paul told us how to go out and fight the battle and how to put on the whole armor of God. Peter warned that we would be tempted, and Christ said in this world we will have tribulation. Paul warned that you must go through many tribulations to enter into the kingdom of God. First Peter was written to teach us that we would suffer, but that we would win if we trusted God. The book of Revelation tells us of those who overcome.

Does anybody preach on overcoming anymore? Is not this a good evangelical doctrine? Or are we so afraid that we will distract from the glory of grace that we are no longer teaching people that they must overcome? We have to be overcomers, and to do so there must be a fight.

"Must I be carried to the skies on flowery beds of ease, while others fight to win the prize and sail through bloody seas? Are there no foes for me to face?" ("Am I a Soldier of the Cross?" Isaac Watts).

Obviously, there is an enticement from sinners. It does not say in Proverbs 1:10, "If sin entices thee." It says, "If sinners entice thee."

The Scripture draws a very sharp distinction here. Sinners are the incarnation of some kind of sin, and sin can hurt you in the abstract. We think of sin as being a sort of evil disembodied vampire bat floating around, and we say, "If sin entices thee," but the Bible does not present it that way. Sin cannot do much until it is incarnated in some sinner, and so it is the sinner who is dangerous. So sin becomes dangerous when it is embodied in a popular figure, a companion, a loved one, or in society.

Sin Embodied in Popular Figures

Sin becomes particularly dangerous when embodied in a popular figure. That is why I am so dead set against everything that emanates from Hollywood. They ask, "Do you think every woman in Hollywood is a harlot?" No. "Do you think every man there is a scoundrel?" No. "Do you think there are no decent homes there?" I think nothing of the sort.

But millions of young people in this country are seeking to look and act like actors and actresses. Vast numbers in the career of acting are working on spouse number four or five. Many of them live corrupt lives, but give the impression that they are not. They are set up as moral examples for our young people.

That is why I claim Hollywood is a cesspool of iniquity, because it embodies sin in popular figures and sets them up as examples for our young people.

Sin Embodied in a Companion

If someone is doing something across town, it will not generally affect you. But when a close companion is involved, and they say, "Come on, let's go and do thus and so," that's where the danger comes in. It is the power of suggestion. It is easier to go along with a good friend.

If sin were always embodied in someone that looked like the devil, with horns and a dark, fallen countenance, it would be no temptation at all. But the temptation to sin is stronger when embodied in nice people whom we generally know and trust. I know many nice, decent people, pleasant to be around, too courteous to argue with you, even about religion. They are just nice people, but if sin is embodied in them, they have a tremendous influence upon those around them.

Sin Embodied in a Loved One

The more you love someone, the more you are going to excuse their wrongdoings and try somehow to extenuate or cover up their behavior.

If sin were just floating around out there, I would not worry. When I first became a Christian, I was afraid of demons or dark spirits, or whatever you want to call them. I do not know much about them. I know some people are devil-conscious to the point of whenever something bad happens they say the devil did it or was to blame. I am not devil-conscious because I am not afraid of the devil anymore; that is, until he is incarnated in someone whom I love or admire. Then I am concerned.

Sin Embodied in Society

Sin becomes dangerous in a society where the mere power of suggestion is influential.

The whole American economy relies upon the power of suggestion. If a law were passed by Congress that said you could not advertise any product, our country would probably collapse overnight. Sales depend upon advertising, which depends upon the power of suggestion. A product is not advertised just once, but again and again and again. They promote it until it becomes a part of our lives—a necessity.

It is perfectly natural for us to walk into a store and immediately reach for something that we have seen advertised. Just handling the item increases the chances of our purchasing it. This pull is so strong that corporations can afford to spend not hundreds, but millions of dollars in advertising. That is the power of suggestion. It can be almost like the power of hypnotism.

Scripture reminds us, "If sinners entice thee, consent thou not" (Proverbs 1:10). Somewhere we have developed the idea that the Christian must be agreeable in everything. We must wear a constant smile, avoid offense, and try to get along with everybody. But that is not what Scripture teaches. The saints in Bible times were usually just two steps short of either jail or the gallows. As a rule, God's people were not liked. If you are a Christian and you are not in some kind of conflict with society, then chances are you are not a very good Christian. The idea that a Christian is always sweet and agreeable, and after he dies they can say of him that he did not have an enemy, is false.

There are really two brotherhoods: the brotherhood of the redeemed and the brotherhood of the unredeemed. The unredeemed divide themselves up into a thousand divisions, but they are still unredeemed. There are two races: Adam was of the first and Jesus Christ is of the second, the head. The redeemed man belongs to the second race, called out of the first race and called unto Christ, and therefore has no fellowship with the first, except the ordinary fellowship of living in the world.

You cannot leave the world; you have to work and live in it, buy and sell and accept the services of and work for and with people in the world, and quite often those people are not right with God. So there is no real fellowship there. To me, brotherhood with the world is all poppycock.

I would like to tell you what you are going to get when you are converted and believe in Christ. It will not always be easy. There will be temptation and trial and disappointment. I would be lying if I told you that you will enter a peaceful, sealed cabin with sweet music and constant fellowship and will one day float on a pink cloud to heaven.

One of the greatest curses of the modern evangelical movement, in my opinion, is that we are somehow becoming "popular." Just as soon as you become popular, something goes out of your life, or more accurately, something has gone out of your life before you get popular.

Historically, the Christian had to be emphatic. He had two words: *yea* or *nay*. When God was talking to him, he said yes, and when the devil was talking to him he said no. When God said, "Do this," he said, "Yes, Lord." When sinners tempted him to stray, he said an emphatic no.

The trouble with us now is that we are double-minded. That is why we are weak. Scripture speaks of the double-minded man. He is "unstable in all his ways" (James 1:8). Elijah illustrated this when he said, "How long halt ye between two opinions? if the Lord be God, follow him: but if Baal, then follow him" (1 Kings 18:21). We need to be on one side or the other. Wholly committed to our high calling in Christ Jesus.

ALL THAT I AM I OWE TO THEE

Search me, O God, my heart discern;
try me, my inmost thought to learn;
and lead me, if in sin I stray,
to choose the everlasting way.
The Psalter, 1912

16

The Warning
of Divine Wisdom

Eternal God and Father of our Lord Jesus Christ, I praise Thee for Thy patience in dealing with my inconsistencies. I trust Thee today with my sincere commitment to follow Thee in all my ways. Amen.

I have found through the years that Christians by the thousands are not wholly committed to Christ. In the Bible we have many examples of this. What I want to find out is why.

First, there was Balaam, in the Bible, who was not wholly committed. He wanted to serve Jehovah, but he also wanted the money that Balak had for him, so he wavered between serving God and serving Balak. When he was over on God's side, he said some beautiful things, such as "There shall come a Star out of Jacob" (Numbers 24:17) and "Let me die the death of the righteous." But when he got over on the other side, he was in sin. He died fighting against God. In the end, he was an uncommitted man.

Balaam had not learned to say yes and no. In fact, a donkey had to talk to him and set him straight (Numbers 22). God Almighty actually turns the irony loose on that prophet and allows a long-eared donkey to rebuke the madness of the prophet. The donkey saw the angel, and the prophet could not see him. At first impulse, he wanted to kill the donkey.

Then the donkey said, "What have I ever done to you? You have ridden me ever since I was big enough for you to ride and now you want to slay me. Why?"

"Oh," he said, "excuse me, I'm sorry, I didn't see the angel."

He was an uncommitted person who could not keep his mind made up. Unfortunately, there are so many people like that today. Even though they might be nice people, like Balaam turned out to be.

Then there was Samson, another man who was uncommitted (Judges 13–16). He walked a tightrope between good and evil. Always one foot on God's side and the other foot on the devil's side; he never quite knew where he was going to turn.

Then, in the New Testament, we have the rich young ruler (Luke 18:18–23). He came to Jesus by night and asked how he could be saved, which showed he was on the side of the Lord. But when the Lord told him how to be saved, he turned his back and showed he was on the side of sin. He was uncommitted.

Then, remember, in the sixth chapter of John after Jesus had given that beautiful talk on the bread of life, some turned back and followed Him no more. Jesus wanted to get to the root of it, so He turned around and said to His disciples, "Will ye also go away?" Peter answered, "Lord, to whom shall we go? thou hast the words of eternal life" (John 6:67–68). So Jesus salvaged some, but many walked away.

They were uncommitted, and there is still the danger of being uncommitted. You might say, "Well, I'm not a very strong Christian, but I do believe the Bible." But the voice of wisdom warns about your being uncommitted. It warns that if you are not committed, the first strong salesman from the other side may win you over.

Many people have gone into a prayer room, knelt, prayed, and got up, but in the end, they did not follow through with their commitment. They went back and picked up their life as it was before.

Again, let me say that these uncommitted people are at the mercy of the strongest salesman, the strongest power of suggestion that comes their way. Consequently, some have wrecked their lives. How could they have saved themselves? "My son, walk not thou in the way with them; refrain thy foot from their path: For their feet run to evil, and make haste to shed blood" (Proverbs 1:15–16). If they had had the ability to say an emphatic no and make it stick, they would have found strength in God to continue in the path of righteousness.

Nobody that stands between you and Jesus Christ is your friend, even your spouse or your father or mother. If that person stands between you and Jesus Christ, that person is not your friend. You must stand for Christ.

Some people are saying, "I believe that in the end everybody will be saved. Everyone will go to heaven." But God will not catch men and drag them to heaven screaming in protest. No one who intentionally follows in the path of sin would be comfortable in heaven.

Hell is the place of moral fools. It is the place for people who could not say yes or no. And Jesus said, "So then because thou art lukewarm, and neither cold nor hot, I will spew thee out of my mouth" (Revelation 3:16). You are either for God or you are against Him.

"The fear of the Lord is the beginning of knowledge: but fools despise wisdom and instruction" (Proverbs 1:7).

Let me repeat that the way of the pilgrim is the way of peril, and you have to learn to say no to the sinner and to temptation when it assails you. Even if it is your closest friend who would lead you astray, you have to say yes to God. I would have more respect for a young man who would walk out of a conversation with me and say, "I'm not on God's side. I'm a sinner, and I'm going to live like one," than for someone who says they will walk in God's way and turns around and walks in his own way and denies any commitment he may have made toward God.

Time is running out and the world is growing old. Dangers are getting sharper and keener, and judgment draws near. Whose side are you on? Where do you stand today?

It is a matter of true commitment to God. Not just playing around; you must commit yourself completely and absolutely to Jesus Christ. Commit yourself, by the grace of God, beyond going back. Burn bridges beyond any possibility of retreat. Be like Elisha, when Elijah called him. Elisha took the wood of his plow to make a fire and used the oxen that had pulled the plow to make a feast so there was no place for him to go back to (see 1 Kings 19:21).

HOW GREAT THE WISDOM

How great the wisdom, power and grace,
Which in redemption shine!
The heavenly host with joy confess
The work is all divine.

Benjamin Beddome

17

Moral Wisdom
vs. Divine Wisdom

O God, my sin has been the destruction of my joy down through the years. My heart is sick with my sin, and I hate that sin and confess it to Thee without any limit on my part. My repentance rests upon Thy gracious forgiveness based upon the blood of the Lord Jesus Christ. Amen.

I see only two ways of viewing mankind: the way man looks at himself and the way God looks at him. If we follow the herd mentality, we will continue to think of ourselves as men generally think of themselves and view ourselves that way.

But if we are wise, we will try to think of ourselves as God thinks of us and see ourselves as God sees us, beginning with the earliest part of the Bible and continuing on to the voice of the patriarchs and prophets and apostles, all the way to Christ himself.

We see God's way of looking at man as a fallen race from the first sin. I do not want to be wise above what is written, but I believe it quite impossible to be a Christian in any more than the most elementary sense of the word without believing that God sees us as a fallen race, fallen from our original position. When man commits a sin against God, we must say he has committed it against himself. This is the terrible irony of sin, that when we sin against God, we sin also against ourselves. When we sin against our fellow man, we sin against God. And when we sin against ourselves, we sin against God: "Against thee, and thee only, have I sinned, and done this evil in thy sight" (Psalm 51:4).

That is the way God sees us. A man sees himself quite differently. He sees himself as a very wise and wonderful being. If he is educated, he sees himself as someone who has crawled up out of an impossible position, fought his way up by some impulse within, and is now pretty well advanced. That is, if he can keep from committing suicide with one of his inventions. He is worried about himself only because he thinks very highly of himself.

That is man's way of looking at himself, but God's way is quite another altogether. A Christian is one who sees himself as God sees him and is not too much influenced by man's way of looking at himself.

And so every man must come over onto God's side, the side of wisdom. You must hear the voice of wisdom calling you over to God's side. You must begin to believe about yourself that you are a fallen man, alienated from the life of God, without hope and without God in the world, driven

by strong passions and filled with frustrations and contradictions—continuing to commit sins against your fellow
man and against yourself, which turn out to be sins against
God. No man sins against himself or against his fellow man
without first sinning against God, or in the same act sinning
against God. That is the way God sees the human race.

Many have refused to accept this and reject the Word of
God and the Lord Jesus Christ. However, there is a happy
side to this. There is a voice calling:

> How long, ye simple ones, will ye love simplicity? and the
> scorners delight in their scorning, and fools hate knowledge?
> Turn you at my reproof: behold, I will pour out my spirit
> unto you, I will make known my words unto you. Because I
> have called, and ye refused; I have stretched out my hand, and
> no man regarded; but ye have set at nought all my counsel,
> and would none of my reproof.
>
> Proverbs 1:22–25

This voice is calling us to return to the wisdom of the just.
There must be an affinity here. "I love them that love me;
and those that seek me early shall find me" (Proverbs 8:17). I
believe that we have degenerated tremendously in our concep-
tion of Christianity because we have taken the rescue mission
as our norm and the figure of speech of paying a debt with
a bank, buying someone out of the market; we have taken
a figure of speech and have twisted it into a doctrine. So
we have commercialized and rationalized Christianity into
the concept that we are debtors and Christ came to pay the
debts, and He did. That is the odd part about this, He did.
When we sing, "Jesus paid it all, all to him I owe; sin had left

a crimson stain, he washed it white as snow" ("Jesus Paid It All," Elvina M. Hall), we are singing the truth.

But I believe that this has been twisted into a lifeboat creed, with Jesus rushing in to save us from hell (and that is true). Man is on the road to hell, and if he is converted, he reverses his direction, and the next thing he knows he will find himself on his way to heaven. All that is true, but I hear the voice of Jesus Christ calling, and not in the language of the marketplace. Rather, I hear the ancient voice of Eternal Wisdom, the one who once wept on the breast of His mother, speaking out of the ancient past. He says to men who have sinned in their folly, "Turn ye unto me, you foolish ones and ye simple ones, for why will ye die?" and says, "I love them that love me." There must be a restoration of affinity.

Christ is that ancient, most excellent wisdom incarnated in our nature and making atonement for all our moral infamy. Any emphasis that makes sin less infamous than that is not biblical. Any interpretation of grace and mercy that allows sin to appear even reasonably excusable in the eyes of God is not a proper interpretation. Any doctrine, any view of sin that allows it to be excused in any way is not biblical. It is not God's way of looking at it, for God looks at sin as *alienation*. God looks at sin as a slap in the divine face and a white-faced angry marching out of the presence of God into the darkness. God sent His only Son to make atonement for our infamy and saves those that turn to the wisdom of the just through repentance.

Now, what is repentance? Satan has managed to put into the mind of Bible Christians that repentance is not a New Testament doctrine, that somehow by the power of grace, repentance is now unnecessary. I think when he did that he accomplished a greater feat of destroying the true faith than all the liberals in the last generation have done! It is dangerous to teach that repentance is not a New Testament doctrine.

We hear Paul say that he is the chief of sinners, not worthy to be converted, and, "Depart from me; for I am a sinful man, O Lord" (Luke 5:8). All those who are sincerely Christian down through the ages have taken the same attitude. They have beaten on their breasts and cried out, "My God, my God, what shall I do? My sins, my sins, my Savior, they take such a hold on me." This has been the true voice of Christianity.

There is only one way to deal with yourself and with sin, and that is to pray that God Almighty will give you a sense of sin sickness, a sickness unto death. I wonder how many there are who have truly been converted, who have not been first sick unto death? Their sins have made them sick. I do not know if it is psychologically possible to believe unto salvation in Christ unless it has been preceded by a sickness unto death, a sense of iniquity and inward infamy that curdles the blood and makes the heart sick.

ERE GOD HAD BUILT THE MOUNTAINS

And couldst Thou be delighted
With creatures such as we,
Who, when we saw Thee, slighted,
And nailed Thee to a tree?
Unfathomable wonder,
And mystery divine!
The voice that speaks in thunder,
Says, "Sinner, I am thine!"

William Cowper

18

Turning from Moral Folly
to Wisdom

*O heavenly Father, for too long I lived according to my
own wisdom and found no rest or peace. Thy eternal
wisdom has brought me to this marvel of repentance
through Jesus Christ, which has brought Thy peace
into my life. Amen.*

We must understand repentance from God's point
of view. Repentance is to seek to become a new
person. It is not simply to get peace, for you
can have peace and be the same person you were. It is not
to get a ticket to heaven. A Christian is not one who has a
ticket to heaven as one might have a ticket to a ball game. A
Christian is one who has sought to become a new person.
He has found himself out and has learned what a scoundrel
he is by the illumination of the Holy Spirit.

He hates what he has been and seeks to be another person altogether—a redeemed person transformed by Christ. That is the repentance found in the Scriptures, particularly the Psalms and the Gospels. It is found in the young man who left home with his inheritance, the prodigal son. It is found in the testimony of Paul. It is found in the language of all the church fathers down through the ages. Repentance is a desire to be a different person.

Some have made Christianity out to be a badge for someone who wants to be a buddy of God. Repentance, however, is to want change, to be another person altogether. Repentance wishes to walk out of oneself, see ourself as a new creature, and when the work of God is fully done, we are a new person: "Therefore if any man be in Christ, he is a new creature: old things are passed away; behold, all things are become new" (2 Corinthians 5:17).

The Marks of True Repentance

Repentance is to seek to become a new person, to open the heart to the incoming of moral wisdom, to seek to be like that most excellent wisdom. It is to seek to live and have an affinity toward Jesus Christ the Lord. The idea that Christ reaches out to you with a lifeboat and pulls you aboard without changing you or identifying himself with you or you with Christ is a modern heresy that ought to be set aside until the Lord comes, or until men learn better.

Moral wisdom cannot save a fool. Moral wisdom can only turn and save the fool who turns from his folly to the wisdom of the just. Not all the infinite value and virtue of the grace of Christ can save a fool who continues in his foolishness.

The one who says he wants to be saved but has no interest in being changed cannot be saved. To be saved, one must care about being like Christ. He will be anxious to be free from sin and alive unto God.

A Moral Fool

Any man who says, "I want to escape judgment, but I do not want to be honest" is a moral fool. He says things like "My business requires that I cut corners, and I want to honor that." He has never heard the tender voice of excellent wisdom say, "Turn unto me. Why will ye continue in your simplicity?" And the man who says, "I want to be God's child, but I can't stop lying to save face" is a moral fool, and God cannot save that man as long as he remains in his folly.

The man who says, "I want to go to heaven, but I don't want to live a pure life; I want to be free to continue with my present life. I will change a little and do better, but I have no desire to be pure," or the man who says, "I want to escape hell and make heaven my home at last, but I have no particular desire to cease to live as I have lived" is deceiving himself.

You are hearing the language of a moral fool. This is not the language of wisdom, but the folly of the damned. For Scripture says, "No man can serve two masters: for either he will hate the one, and love the other; or else he will hold to the one, and despise the other. Ye cannot serve God and mammon" (Matthew 6:24).

I believe the doctrine of grace and justification by faith with all my heart and preach them consistently and regularly. To anyone who would twist these doctrines and turn

Christianity into a kind of arm's length salvation, God says, "I love them that love me; and those that seek me early shall find me" (Proverbs 8:17).

The penitent man wants to be changed. If you are still sufficiently in love with yourself and all you want is a little improvement, I see no possibility of faith approaching your heart. Unless a man comes to Christ seeking to be a different person, to be humble, meek, and self-effacing, he is not coming to Christ at all. Unless we hate evil and love righteousness, at least to the degree we are able at the moment, we are still in the bonds of iniquity and the enemies of righteousness.

To be repentant means to come to Christ self-accusing and without defense. Whenever we throw up a defense of our lives and say, "I'm not as bad as other men," there is no faith involved. To say rather, "I have sinned, I am without excuse," there is the language of the penitent man, the language of that ancient wisdom.

A man wants to be saved, modest, pure, and temperate. Some say he must have these qualities before he is converted. No, he must be a seeker of these qualities. He must throw his heart open to receive these qualities.

I know it is impossible for a speckled bird to change its speckles. I know no one can change the color of their skin, and I know that God does not expect us to be righteous on our own. If we were righteous, He would not have had to die to save us. But being unrighteous, we must make the choice to turn back toward righteousness and set our affections and our face toward it. Like the prodigal son, we will reverse our direction and start back toward God. I believe the truly penitent man will be weary of this world and the things of this world, and will be longing after God and eternal wisdom.

If your concept of Christianity is simply to escape hell, I will not say positively there is no hope for you, but I would say that you have not heard the voice of the Holy Spirit yet, the voice of eternal wisdom that calls men to repent and be changed.

Oh, I want to be other than what I am. I want to be different. I want to change. I am not satisfied. I want to believe in Thee, and trust in Thee, and throw myself boldly on Thee, and I want to be made like Thyself. I do not want only to escape hell, I want to escape sin. I not only want to go to heaven at last, but I want to have heaven in my heart now. I not only want to dwell with the redeemed, I want to be like the redeemed here on the earth. I want to be another kind of person. That is the prayer of repentance, and if we do not agree, I do not believe we know what repentance is all about.

Henry Suso was a German saint who wrote a book that included a prayer he made at the beginning of his Christian life:

Sweet and tender Lord! From the days of my childhood, my mind has sought for something with burning thirst, but what it is I have not as yet fully understood.

We have a concept of childhood as being completely careless. We say, "We all should be like children. They have no fears, no longings, no regrets."

How many can say, from the days of your childhood, you were like that? Maybe you were not brought up in a Christian home. Maybe you did not go to a gospel church. Maybe you had no chance, no light at all, but in your heart, even as a kid, there was a longing for something. Suso prayed,

> Lord, what that is, I cannot yet fully understand. Lord, I have pursued it for many years eagerly and I have never yet succeeded because I do not know rightly what it is and yet it is something that draws my soul toward it and without which I know I can never find true peace.

So while he lived on earth, his heart was open to the voice of God. Suso heard the voice of the gospel without ever having been to a church. "That was the true Light, which lighteth every man that cometh into the world" (1 John 1:0). And Suso knew that without having what he sought he would have no peace.

Could you say that without knowing the gospel or much of the Bible at all? Maybe even now there is a longing after something that draws your soul. Maybe you have suppressed the feeling in your heart. You get busy in school or at work. You read other things, listen to the radio, watch television, go to baseball games, and you try to cover it up. It is there, nevertheless, and you know it is there, and it has been there all the time.

Maybe you look for it in a boyfriend, a girlfriend, or in one affair after another, and you have not found it. You may look for it in the things you possess, but as soon as you are alone, you know that is not it.

You try to find it in sports, money, or a good job. You try to find it in education. "I tried to find it in other people," Suso recalled, "as I saw what others seemed to have, but the more I sought it the less I found, and the closer I seemed to come, the farther off it was." It is amazing that someone could so describe our hearts. No, it is not so amazing, because we are all alike.

IMMORTAL, INVISIBLE, GOD ONLY WISE

Unresting, unhasting, and silent as light,
nor wanting, nor wasting, thou rulest in might:
thy justice, like mountains high soaring above,
thy clouds which are fountains of goodness and love.
                                        Walter C. Smith

19

The Voice of Wisdom
Calling Us Back

I praise Thee, O God, for the restlessness of my spirit
has driven me forward to discover my rest completely
in Thee. I seek Thee, O God, and nothing more. Amen.

The world is divided into two classes: the Esaus and the Jacobs.

Esau is a man of the earth, a finished and finite clod, untroubled by a spark, seemingly without a conscience, without a longing after God, without ever having heard the voice of eternal wisdom.

Jacob is crooked, wicked, subtle, and dissimilar as can be, but has a longing in his heart. But what he seeks is not always righteous. For twenty years Jacob cheated his father-in-law; twenty years he had wives and begat children; twenty years he was an old scoundrel there in the household of Laban. But all the time God was saying to Jacob, "This is not what thou seekest."

Have you ever heard the voice within you about the time you thought, *If I could just get this, it will be wonderful?*

I have had young brides come and tell me of the terror within their hearts and how utterly lost they were and how utterly disappointed. Not in their husband, per se, but they thought that marriage would be it. If a woman could find the man of her dreams and get married, that is what she was born for.

So she walks up the aisle to the smell of roses and the sound of music, and when it is all over, she says, "O God, this isn't it. I love him and he's a wonderful man and I don't feel worthy of him, but this isn't what I thought it would be."

The young man gets his PhD, and says, "O God, this isn't all there is." Another man buys an expensive car, and as he contemplates his good fortune, he cries, "My God, this isn't it, is it?"

How I thank God from the depths of my soul that He always followed me around and always troubled me. How I praise God forever and ever that I have always been a troubled man. I start to settle down to something, and God says, "That isn't it."

Henry Suso wrote, "I have a revulsion for *things*, and all the joy and fun in the world is not it. My heart yearns for it, for I would gladly possess it, and I have often experienced what it is not, but what it is my heart has not yet discovered." What a prayer for a man to make.

Suso wrote beautiful hymns and books of devotion as well. This is how it began, and then he heard the voice say, "It is

I, Eternal Wisdom, who, with the embrace of my eternal providence, have chosen thee in eternity for myself alone. I have barred the way to thee as often as thou wouldst have parted company with me, had I permitted thee. In all things thou didst ever meet with some obstacle, and it is the sweet sign of my elect that I will needs have them for myself."

The man who wrote this heard the voice of God say through the Scriptures, "Henry, it is I," for a few lines further on it turned out to be Christ who was talking all the time, so he began to talk back to the Lord Jesus. He found this ancient wisdom; it was talking to him and was none other than what Paul said, "In whom dwelleth all wisdom." So it turns out that it was Christ, and He said to him, "It is I you have been seeking. That is what you have wanted all these years and could not find, eternal wisdom, and the reason you wanted me was that I have chosen thee." Hear that now, whatever your doctrine or creed, hear that: "Ye have not chosen me, but I have chosen you, and ordained you."

Esau cannot hear it. It's as if his ears are plugged up with red clay. He is born out of the clay, he lives on the clay; he'll die and be buried in the clay and rise terrified to stand in judgment before his God. But every Jacob, crooked and sinful and bad as he may be, has within him something that responds to the call of the gospel. God says of him, "Fear not, O Jacob, my servant . . . whom I have chosen" (Isaiah 44:2).

It is terrible to be content with things, ambitions, hopes, and dreams that laugh in your face. Hopes that will disappoint you, and you will hear the hollow laughter when it is too late. Jesus said, "I love them that love me; and those that seek me early shall find me" (Proverbs 8:17). He is the wisdom of the Old Testament and the New, and He is calling you.

I do not want to put you under pressure. I only want you to think soberly and gravely about your life. If you have been troubled with the vanity of it all, I can tell you where to find what you were born for. "Come unto me, all ye that labour and are heavy laden, and I will give you rest" (Matthew 11:28). It is the voice of Jesus calling, the voice of that ancient eternal wisdom calling you back from the folly of the fool to the wisdom of the just. Away from what you are to what you want to be, away from yesterday to a glorious tomorrow—and you can start right now. For He said, "Behold, I stand at the door, and knock: if any man hear my voice, and open the door, I will come in to him, and will sup with him, and he with me" (Revelation 3:20). Wherever the gospel invitation goes, you can hear it: "Come unto me."

I often think of the church bell in the country. Sunday morning, about 10:30, it is ringing. The farmers are gathering from everywhere, and that bell is saying, "Come, come, come." The man who wrote "Church in the Wildwood" (Dr. William S. Pitts, 1857) evidently thought of that. It is what the church bell is saying; it is the call of the gospel; it is Jesus' call to every man who will hear.

Come away from yourself, seek to be a changed person, and do not try to make terms with God. Do not say merely, "I want to be saved," but, say, "*O Jesus, my heart sought something that I yearned for and didn't know where to find, but now I know what it is. Thou hast chosen me to be thine own and the reason I couldn't settle down and be content with my gifts and riches and treasures is that Thou hast selected me and troubled me until I found Thee.*"

Thank God that He troubled you. Better to be a troubled Jacob than a disturbed, frustrated, and resistant Esau.

❦ O LORD, THY ALL DISCERNING EYES ❦

Before, behind, I meet Thine eye,
And feel Thy heavy hand:
Such knowledge is for me too high,
To reach or understand:
What of Thy wonders can I know?
What of Thy purpose see?
Where from Thy Spirit shall I go?
Where from Thy presence flee?

John Q. Adams

20

The Voice of Wisdom
Calls for a Choice

Dear heavenly Father, may I set before me only that
which will glorify Thee in all the beauty of Thy purity
and holiness. I pray Thy wisdom will guide me through-
out my life in making the choices that will bless me and
honor Thee. Amen.

Hear a voice here, the voice of wisdom speaking—
the voice of the beautiful *Sophia*, whom the church
fathers called Excellent Wisdom.

This beautiful Sophia is older than the firstborn sons of
light, and as the poet said in another setting, "Time writes
no wrinkle on thine azure brow, such as creation's dawn
beheld, thou rollest now" ("The Ocean," Lord Byron). For
she is coeternal with God; as we have labored to show, this

wisdom, though seen here as female, is none other than Jesus Christ our Lord, conceived of the Holy Ghost and born of the Virgin Mary. All wisdom became incarnated in that mortal flesh.

This wisdom is concerned with man. She says, "My son" over and over in the book of Proverbs, and I wonder why God is concerned with lost men. He was not so concerned with lost angels, for in Jude 1:6 it says, "And the angels which kept not their first estate, but left their own habitation, he hath reserved in everlasting chains under darkness unto the judgment of the great day." There is not one shadow of light falling across the stringent darkness of that prism where lie the fallen angels.

Sometimes I wonder why for man there is redemption, yet for fallen angels there is none. He did not say, "Let us make angels in our image." It was when He created man that he said, "Let us make man in our image, after our likeness" (Genesis 1:26), which made us infinitely dear to God.

Christian mystic and theologian Julian of Norwich, said, "For our soul is so preciously loved of him that is highest, that it over-passes the knowing of all creatures." In truth, no human alive can fathom how much, how sweetly and tenderly, our Maker loves us. Therefore, we stand, spiritually holding with everlasting marvel this high, over-passing, inestimable love that the Almighty God in His goodness has for us, and the reason is that He made us in His image and so made possible the incarnation of Jesus. He was made in the image of man because man had been made in the image of God.

That means men are redeemable and angels and demons are not. With all our pains, disappointments, sorrows, heart-aches, grief, and losses, I am glad that I was born of the human family. I am glad that I was not born an angel or created an angel. I am glad that I was born a man of the seed of Adam and of the human race.

Notice what God calls us to, for this is the voice of God, the voice of the beautiful, all-excellent wisdom, the voice of the Lord Jesus Christ, and the voice of the Holy Ghost. He is calling us to himself. In Proverbs 2:5, He is calling us to the fear of the Lord. That is to reverential awe and an ability to worship. This is what He calls us to.

The *fear of the Lord* is a beautiful term, and I do not think it needs to be explained, but some have wondered why God would have us fear Him. He has us fear Him because of who He is, but the fear we feel is not the chilling and corrosive fear sinners feel for death or judgment or hell. It is a reverential awe; it is respect, worship, and the knowledge of God. He says, "And this is life eternal, that they might know thee, the only true God, and Jesus Christ, whom thou hast sent" (John 17:3).

What does this wisdom call us away from? You can be perfectly sure that if He calls us toward anything, He calls us away from its opposite. If you are moving toward something, you are moving away from the opposite. If you are going south, you have your back turned to the north. If you are moving toward heaven, you have your back turned toward hell. If you are moving toward God, you have your back turned toward the devil. You can be sure if you are moving toward righteousness, you have your back turned toward sin. So if He is calling us to the fear of the Lord and the knowledge of God, what is He calling us away from? Proverbs 2:12–16 tells us that He calls us away from the way of the evil man and from the strange woman.

What is the way of the evil man? The Bible uses a great many figures of speech, and the word *way* is one of those figures of speech. It means a highway, a path, a road, a lane away through to something, and the way of the evil man is the path he is following. This is the direction he is taking, but it does not mean a geographical path. It means a path of light, a moral path, a path of conduct, and it says that the evil man leaves the path of righteousness and walks in the way of darkness and rejoices to do evil, and his ways are crooked and his paths perverse.

This is God's description of man. He leaves the paths of righteousness and walks in the way of darkness; he rejoices to do evil, his ways are crooked and his paths perverse. God loves to talk about a straight way and a crooked way, another analogy, but it's a great way. It says of the creatures in the Old Testament, the first chapter of Ezekiel, that everyone went straight forward. Then when he went, he went straight forward, no banking and circling, turning, diving, and ducking, but every one of those strange creatures went straight forward. Jesus Christ set His face like a flint, and went straight to the goal. Jesus said that the man who goes to heaven will go the straight way, but the broad way, the crooked way, is the way to hell, and this man has left that way. His ways are crooked, he walks in the way of darkness, and his paths are perverse.

How did he get this power over people? He gets it by the power of the example of this man, of whom the Holy Ghost writes and of whom wisdom speaks. He is not a vicious fellow with a leather jacket and a switchblade. Do not think of him in that way at all. He is a hero, and in some ways he may be a very noble fellow and much could be said that is good about him from the human standpoint. So let us not think that if things get bad enough nobody would follow him.

The power to subvert, seduce, persuade, and lead away depends in a large measure upon the attractiveness of the person whose example we follow. Nobody sets out to follow a bum on the street who smells of the garbage heap. Nobody sets out deliberately to follow the man who is going to a gas chamber or to be hanged for his crime. But if he succeeds in making himself something of a smooth, pleasant, and attractive man, he leads men astray. Just how does he do it? He does it by the power of example, and where does example get its power over us? It is our incurable bent to imitate that gives example its power.

Millions in hell are there who simply could not resist imitating others. They did not intend to do it, that is, they did not plan to go to hell, but were too weak to resist; they imitated. So that there are some who smoke, not that they ever cared for it, but they could not resist imitating those who did. Some who drink alcohol may have been terribly sick of it and did not like it, but they could not resist imitating those who drank. Some use foul language because they cannot resist reflecting and echoing the voices they hear.

The evil man, the man who may be well-dressed, with slick hair and driving a big car, nevertheless has left the paths of righteousness to walk in the way of darkness. People look at him and think he must really be on top of the world. And so if he swears, they swear, if he drinks, they drink, if he lies, they lie, if he's rowdy, they are rowdy, and if he's rebellious, they are rebellious, and if he steals, they will steal. So we have people going astray because they cannot resist the power of imitation. Thousands are imitating themselves into hell because they simply cannot resist it. It is the response of their heart to that which they admire.

That is why it is so important that we should admire the right thing as well as the right person, the right kind of person. Everybody is going to try to be like the person or behavior they admire.

Years ago, there were books in the schools called the *Mc-Guffey Readers*. They glorified goodness, made heroes out of good men, and a generation or two of strong, sound, robust Americans grew up reading the McGuffey Readers because they placed heroes before us that were noble men and women. It was not the wooden heroes of modern fiction, which nobody believes in, but they were real persons, individuals in history, and they turned the eyes of a whole generation or more toward righteousness. They put the right model before us.

Better to pick the right model. Better to be sure you are trying to be like somebody who is worthwhile, because the power of imitation is inescapable. We cannot get away from it. If we admire anybody, we are going to try to be like them. That is why I believe Christians ought to read Christian biographies; we ought to inform ourselves in Christian history and church history. That is why we ought to become acquainted with the best people and follow them. We are imitators, and the evil man has tremendous influence over generations of young people, because they admire him and they admire what they believe is his success. The result is that what they imitate they will soon be like.

The Holy Spirit says of ancient wisdom,

If you will listen and understand righteousness, and judgment, and equity, and every good path, wisdom will enter into your heart, and knowledge will enter your soul. Then it shall preserve your understanding, shall keep you and deliver you from the way of the evil man who leaves the path of uprightness to walk in the way of darkness.

Paraphrase of Proverbs 2

IMMORTAL, INVISIBLE, GOD ONLY WISE

Great Father of glory, pure Father of light,
Thine angels adore Thee, all veiling their sight;
But of all Thy rich graces this grace, Lord, impart
Take the veil from our faces, the vile from our heart.

Walter C. Smith

21

The Delivering Power
of Divine Wisdom

O Eternal Wisdom, I trust Thee in all aspects of my life. I turn away from the world in the power the Holy Spirit and choose to follow Thee throughout the rest of my days. I refuse to come under the influence of anything apart from the Holy Spirit. Amen.

In the last chapter, I focused on the evil man, but now I need to deal with the strange woman. Who is this strange woman? "To deliver thee from the strange woman, even from the stranger which flattereth with her words" (Proverbs 2:16).

She is set here dramatically before us as being the exact opposite of the beautiful, all-excellent wisdom. It was common among the old Jews, particularly the highly spiritual ones, to set forth wisdom as the Bible does as the beautiful woman calling men away from evil to the path of light and righteousness and purity. Over against her was the other woman, and compared with the beautiful Sophia, she lacked modesty, meekness, purity, loyalty, gentleness, faithfulness, and moral beauty. There came an example of such a woman one time in Israel. Her name was Jezebel.

She was not a Jewess; she was a Phoenician princess, the daughter of Ethbaal, king of Tyre. (First Kings 16:31 says she was a Zidonian, a biblical term for Phoenicians.) She married Ahab, who was a Jewish Hebrew king, and that woman was exactly the opposite.

You could describe this beautiful woman of the Proverbs as standing at the head of the street calling all the foolish, wayward sons of men to God and righteousness. All of her uprightness, all of her purity, all of her modesty, all of her cleanness, all of her sobriety and soundness, all of her penetrating vision, all of her humility, all this that she had is exactly what Jezebel did not have.

Jezebel was the first lady of the land, and all but damned Israel because the young women of the land tried to be like her. They admired her because she did well. Success was the goddess, and she was worshiping at its shrine, and they were worshiping at her shrine. Here is this woman, the strange woman, no woman really, nobody in particular, but the opposite of this other woman. Just as the other woman is nobody in particular, it is the figure of a charmingly beautiful woman calling sinners away from darkness. Now another figure stands out as strange because it is different from this beautiful woman, different from Sarah, different from

Hannah, different from the sweet, good, home-loving, honest, upright women.

He describes her just as he describes the evil man. She flatters with her words, she has forsaken the teaching of her girlhood, she forgets the covenant of her God, her house inclines toward death, and she leads others astray; she is moral folly personified.

We have them going up and down the land today. They make hundreds of thousands of dollars a year, and their pictures are seen everywhere. They personify the American success in publicity and popularity and high ratings on TV and at the box office. This strange woman knows how to say the smooth thing, and you never catch her blushing. She is long past that. Never catch her saying anything simple. She has to be sophisticated and smart, and if she remembers the Sunday school she used to go to it is only something she has shrugged off and outgrown. She forsakes the teaching of her girlhood. If she remembers the time that she wept at an altar, she would not admit it because she has forgotten the covenant of her God. She is moral folly personified, and the other is most excellent wisdom personified.

How does this woman work? The evil man works with the power of example, the evil woman works by the power of suggestion. Why is suggestion so powerful among men and women today?

Most people do not have their minds made up, which is why advertising is so powerful. If a man had his mind made up that he wanted something, you could not advertise him out of it, but because we always go with our minds open to new things, the advertiser has this tremendous power, this ability to put a suggestion in our minds and we follow it. Many are brainwashed from nine o'clock in the morning or earlier until the last eyelid flutters shut at night because of the power of suggestion. These people are uncommitted. They go through life uncommitted, not sure in which direction they are going.

I think of the many young people who go to certain colleges not because they are called of God to go or because they have any good sound reason, but because somebody they know went there. It is again, the power of suggestion.

Men buy cars not because they are convinced that it is the best car, but because someone they know said, "Oh, you ought to get one. It is the grandest thing." They live in a certain suburb, not because they ever thought of it on their own, but because somebody else moved out there, and suggestion and example were too much for them, so they are up to their eyebrows in debt because they could not resist the suggestion of those who flatter with their words.

The older I get, the more I admire people who are hard to push around. They are going somewhere, they know where they are going, and while they are courteous and nice about it, you are not going to change their minds. They know where they are going, and the man of God or the young person who has found Christ will be settled about it. The strange woman might just as well take her truck and peddle her wares somewhere else, because she will not affect them. There are some, not too many, whom you might just as well let alone or not seek to flatter, because they are unflatterable. Others, who do not have their minds made up, are walking the tightrope, and the result is that all they need is a suggestion.

Did you ever go shopping for clothes and could not decide on something? Finally, your spouse says, "I think you should take this," and a great burden rolled off your shoulders and you bought it. You could not decide, and you were glad to fall back on somebody that would make up your mind for you. That is exactly why advertising is so powerful and why the suggestion of the strange woman is so powerful. They make up your mind and you are relieved of the necessity. I refuse to turn my mind over to anybody.

When the woman ate of the fruit and her eyes were opened, she gave some to her husband, and he ate of it, and then God came around to talk to both of them about it. After being disappointed and not finding them in the garden in the cool of the day, God came to them and He said to the man, "Who persuaded thee?" And he said, "This woman." And he was right. He did not have courage enough on his own. He was the first henpecked husband, the first who would not obey God because of his smiling, pretty wife.

Then God went to her and said, "Who persuaded you?" And she said, "The serpent did." Adam was glad to get the responsibility off his shoulders, turning it over to his wife. She was glad to get rid of it, turning it over to the devil. They passed the buck, and when it reached the serpent, there was no where for it to go after that. So God cursed the serpent, but he did recognize the power of suggestion.

Christianity in our time is trying to get young people who have turned themselves over to the world, to the strange woman, to the incarnation of all that is not good to choose the opposite. But we have a generation that is trying to harmonize Christianity with the world. Some have accepted Christ because they were pressured into it and persuaded by the smooth-talking man who does not really know what he is doing.

The Holy Ghost says, "Incline thine ear" (Proverbs 2:2; 4:20). That is, bend down and listen; apply thine heart and choose the good path.

How sad that we have a generation that would not be caught dead reading this, those who are not interested in true Christianity. How heartbreaking that what put iron in the backbone of a generation of early Americans has now been skipped over and forgotten and called legalistic.

Christ quoted from the book of Proverbs, as did the other writers of the New Testament. Wisdom cries out and moderates her voice. Do you hear it? Do you hear His voice?

Some can still hear the voice of God. I am glad for them. They are the dearest, most wonderful people in the world. When God speaks, they can still their ear and say, "All right, I am getting a signal. I hear the voice of eternal wisdom and He says to me, 'Come away from the strange woman, however beautiful. Come away from the evil man, however well off. Follow the voice of God.'"

This generation will have set before them two ways: The way of God or the way of the world. The way of sin or the way of righteousness. The way of heaven or the way of hell. The way of bad example or the way of good example. Pray that they choose the right way.

ERE GOD HAD BUILT THE MOUNTAINS

When, like a tent to dwell in,
He spread the skies abroad,
And swathed about the swelling
Of Ocean's mighty flood;

He wrought by weight and measure,
And I was with Him then:
Myself the Father's pleasure,
And mine, the sons of men.

William Cowper

22

God's Wisdom Is Justified in the Redeemed

Holy Father, I praise Thee for the wisdom Thou hast poured into my soul, the wisdom to recognize the Lord Jesus Christ as my Savior. Amen.

The wisdom of man and the wisdom of God stand radically opposed to each other.

The city of Corinth was a sort of Boston of its time with a great many Greek philosophers. There was a fine, strong, vigorous church there, and Paul went to that church and preached. He wrote at least two epistles to them, and Paul said to these philosophers,

And I, brethren, when I came to you, came not with excellency of speech or of wisdom, declaring unto you the testimony of God. For I determined not to know any thing among you, save Jesus Christ, and him crucified. And I was with you in weakness, and in fear, and in much trembling. And my speech and my preaching was not with enticing words of man's wisdom, but in demonstration of the Spirit and of power: That your faith should not stand in the wisdom of men, but in the power of God.

1 Corinthians 2:1–5

Then he says further,

But we speak the wisdom of God in a mystery, even the hidden wisdom, which God ordained before the world unto our glory: Which none of the princes of this world knew: for had they known it, they would not have crucified the Lord of glory.

1 Corinthians 2:7–8

That was Paul's opinion. He was not rationalizing or trying to defend himself. This man knew the wisdom of the Greeks and could quote from them at his pleasure as well as the poets. He was a profoundly learned man in addition to being one of the great intellects of all time, and yet he says that the wisdom of man and the wisdom of God stand opposed to each other.

The wisdom of God is a holy thing, an attribute of the holy being of God himself out of which flows the whole universe and the whole scheme of redemption incarnated in Jesus Christ the Lord; He walked the earth wisdom incarnated. Wisdom at whose great sea the wise of the world stood and dipped and took a little, but misunderstood it, misapplied it, took it as their own and thus have become foolish and their foolish hearts were darkened. The wisdom of the world is folly because it is an unholy thing and it is therefore a fatal snare and a delusion.

This sounds old-fashioned, and I know how quickly it can be dismissed. In our day, we have a way of dismissing men with a name. A man makes a statement and we call him neoorthodox. He makes another statement and we say he's a Calvinist. He makes another, and we say he's Armenian or premillenarian or postmillenarian, and thus we tag men. So I know how easily learned men of the world, particularly the learned Evangelicals, can tag me.

The great apostle said that these two wisdoms stand opposed to each other. One is the holy wisdom of God in a mystery, the other is man's little bit of wisdom. One is the great fathomless, shoreless ocean, and the other is a little landlocked lagoon filled with small fish and gummy green stuff because it is evil and less than good.

Jesus noticed children playing in the marketplaces and compared them to these impossible, self-contradictory Pharisees and lawyers who rejected the counsel of God, being not baptized of John. Jesus said of them,

> But whereunto shall I liken this generation? It is like unto children sitting in the markets, and calling unto their fellows, and saying, we have piped unto you and ye have not danced; we have mourned unto you, and ye have not lamented.
>
> Matthew 11:16–17

Jesus came eating and drinking and they accused Him of being a glutton and habitual wine drinker. John the Baptist was somewhat ascetical and came *not* eating and drinking, and they said he had the devil. "You are like children," Jesus told them, "for the children pipe a happy tune and they say, now everybody dance, and then they sing a mournful song and expect everyone to lament."

People are falsely accused by those who do not understand their motives for doing what they do or don't do. Children, in their play, expect grown-ups to follow them in their folly and make-believe.

Jesus said there is no reason for doing either. He accused the Pharisees, religionists, and churchmen of playing at religion. He said they were simply whimsical, illogical, and changeable like children, who can give no reason for anything they are doing.

One of the great fallacies that the Christian has to get over is the fundamentalist fear of education and intellect. There is no intellect anywhere big enough to scare me. Nobody can know enough to discredit the Holy Scriptures or Jesus Christ. You cannot learn enough to prove that Jesus Christ was not God, or that He did not rise from the dead, or that He is not at the right hand of God and coming again in glory. You just cannot know enough.

A dear brother of a generation or two ago confessed that occasionally he had doubts. "When I'm visited by a doubt," he said, "about the Christian faith and worry about the foundations of my faith, I plunge deep into the Book and I search and always come back to the surface singing, 'How firm a foundation ye saints of the Lord is laid for your faith in His excellent word.'"

We must not be afraid of education, and we must not conclude fallaciously that to be dumb is to be spiritual and to be educated is to be unspiritual. That does not follow at all. We have today holy men who are also men of great mental capacity and profound learning. Do not equate spirituality with ignorance, and do not equate unbelief with learning. Always remember, while you do not glorify ignorance you are not taken in by the wisdom of the world, for the wisdom of the world is a fallen and unbelieving thing. It grows out of the stem of Adam. It belongs to a fallen race. It is the best the fallen race has outside of human love, but it is not trustworthy, and whenever anything intersects the wisdom of God, follow the wisdom of God.

The second great fallacy we Christians have to get over is confidence in the wisdom of men, illustrated by confidence in science.

It is amazing to me how the people of the world trust scientists and how much they make of them. Science has done much to bless our culture and we are thankful. Isn't it a strange and ominous thing that the same scientists who have pulled the fangs out of killer diseases also put in the hands of wicked men a tool with which they can wipe the face of the earth clean of humanity and destroy the same men they labored night and day for centuries to save from disease?

Science is a human thing. It is better to wash your face than to be dirty. It is better to live in a clean house than to dwell in a swap. It is better to have human science than to dwell among the witchcraft doctors of Africa, but let nobody for one second imagine that science has the answer to man's deep cry. There is a cry within the human heart; it is a cry after God, a yearning that will never be satisfied by anyone but God.

It is a great fallacy to trust science, a great fallacy to trust politicians. A Christian has to—by the exercise of his mind—violently break himself loose from any confidence in scientists, politicians, philosophers, writers, actors, dramatists, great musicians, or great anything else. They do not have what we want or need. We are not against them; we may love them, but we do not trust them because they do not have what only God has to give us.

Jesus said wisdom is justified of all her children. This wisdom, this trust in God, in Christ is the wisest thing in the world. The Christian turns against the ways of the world and by so doing invites friction, hostility, and sometimes persecution. This is not a blanket indictment against workplaces, but often the Christian will invite hostility, friction, and persecution merely by his lack of participation in conversation or behavior that is unseemly. You are honest and hardworking and you have invited trouble by turning against the opposite behavior.

The greatest military power and civilized nation in the world was the Roman Empire, not a nation but a combination of nations. The greatest religious power in the world was Israel. The two combined to put the man Christ Jesus to death, and He died as a criminal. Yet after the passing of two thousand years, there are yet those who follow His Word and who for His sake invite trouble and persecution, take up a cross and walk on, bearing that cross when they could toss it off their shoulders and fit in. Crazy, huh? Ah, my brethren, what makes the difference? Paul said, "I know whom I have believed," and so do I.

We Christians are a strange crowd. We make more of the invisible than the visible. We talk constantly to someone we cannot see. We act as if things were real that people do not believe are real and waive aside things that some people attach great value to. We sing about a man who was rejected and crucified, and we say, "We find the yoke easy."

I can testify that all my troubles I brought on myself by failing my God, and all that I regret I brought on myself by my sins, and I do not regret one minute I have ever given to God or to His people. Nor do I regret any sacrifice ever made for Him. The only regret I have is not loving Him as much as I should have, for the yoke is indeed easy and the burden is light.

Our confidence is in God, and as such, we invite trouble, but in the meantime, we thank God. Wisdom is justified of her children, and that ancient flowing sea of God's pulsating, creative wisdom moves through His world, touching the consciences of men and whispering, "Come unto me all ye that labour and are heavy laden and I will give you rest."

That ancient wisdom will justify itself in men and women who have given their hearts to Christ and live fully the Christian life. Those who thought they had something, but turned their backs on Jesus, in that awful day when the secrets of men's minds and hearts are made known, they will regret and mourn, and it will be too late.

The servant of God shines forth as the sun in the kingdom of His Father. I want to be in that number when the saints go marching into that kingdom.

☙ HOW GREAT THE WISDOM ❧

They tell the triumphs of His cross,
The sufferings which He bore;
How low He stooped, how high He rose,
And rose to stoop no more.
Benjamin Beddome

23

God's Wisdom Is Absolute and Unqualified (Not Limited)

Most gracious heavenly Father, I long to know Thee as Thou delightest to reveal Thyself to me. Let me know Thee through the magnitude of Thy eternal wisdom. Let my heart be the nesting place of Thy blessed Holy Spirit. Amen.

It is necessary to mental and moral health that we believe in the plenary wisdom of God, that is, the full wisdom of God. God is not permitted to have just a bit of wisdom or almost the sum of all wisdom, but we believe God has all wisdom, full wisdom beyond which there cannot be any wisdom. It is necessary to Christian faith, to mental rest and moral soundness that we believe in this wisdom of God as being absolute, perfect, and infinite, and I am not using words carelessly.

By *absolute* I mean unqualified, not limited. What God is, He is without qualification. God is not a creature, but a Creator. He contains all things, all things are in Him, and therefore when we talk about wisdom, we mean the unqualified wisdom of God. When we talk about God's knowledge, we mean an unqualified knowledge—that God knows everything there is to know and knows it instantaneously and at once and that nothing can be added to what He knows. He cannot be taught anything. He cannot be informed. He knows it all, absolute knowledge, and so with every other attribute of God, every other facet of the perfect diamond of His created nature, everything is absolute.

Then when I say *perfect*, I mean that it admits of no improvement, that you cannot improve the wisdom of God. You could improve David's wisdom; you could improve the wisdom of the sages and saints and mystics and worshipers, but you cannot improve the wisdom of God. If all the created wise beings that the Bible hints at were all to get together and hold a conference, they could not in any way improve on the wisdom of God.

I use the word *infinite* and say it is necessary that we believe in the infinite wisdom of God. *Infinitude*, of course, means it is without bounds or limits, and since the very organ you use to think about it does have bounds and limits, you are trying to make the lesser contain the greater, which is why no one can ever fully understand the infinitude of God. Yet we find in the Scriptures the word *infinite* occurring, and find it in Christian theology, so God's wisdom is absolute in that it is unqualified. It is perfect in that it admits of no improvement, and it is infinite in that it has no bounds or limits. Only God has such wisdom.

We use words very carelessly. For instance, we may talk about an infinite amount of trouble a man went to. There is no such thing as an infinite amount of trouble. There is no such thing as absolute honesty. We say a man is absolutely honest. No, he is just honest, not absolutely honest. Such words can only be said of God. You can only use the word *absolute* when you are referring to God.

When you use the word *infinite*, you must mean God. When you use the word *perfect*, you must be speaking of God. You may use these words in a relative sense, and so we use an unrelated word and unqualified word in a qualified sense and an infinite word in a very limited sense. But, of course, we are playing with language when we do it, because only God has wisdom, for the Scriptures refer to God as only wise (Romans 16:27) and the only wise God our Savior (Jude 25).

When the Holy Ghost said that only God was wise and when He said that our Savior God was the only wise God, He was not using words in the way we do. This was inspired, and so we know that only God has the final wisdom. That is why the Old Testament warns the wise man not to depend upon his own wisdom. That is why Jesus said God has hidden things from the wise and the prudent and revealed them unto babes. That is why Paul, in 1 Corinthians, burned with irony the supposed and self-appointed wise men of his generation and told them they had better humble themselves and know that they know nothing in order that they might know something.

I do not offer proof that God is wise. One of the greatest proofs of our own deep uncertainty within our hearts is when we try to prove God. We do not offer any proof, we utter the word *God* and that is it. We do not have to prove it. If God is what He says He is and what the Bible declares Him to be, and what the worshiping, radiant, rapturous, singing saints have declared Him to be, then we do not have to bring God to the bar of any man's proof and have God stand quietly with His cap in hand and allow us to prove Him. To do so is to insult His majesty and is an affront to the Ancient of Days. Furthermore, the embittered, unbelieving man would never believe any proof anyway, and the worshiping heart does not ask any proof. Jesus said you are blessed because you have seen Him, and that is good, but if you have not seen Him and still believe, you are more blessed.

Either I do believe in God, or I do not. Either I hold God to be wise altogether, or I do not. Either I believe that He is, or I doubt Him. Either I believe that He is the only wise God our Savior, or I do not. Everything lies here: destiny, death, life, heaven, and hell, and the Christian has an answer for the doubter.

I know that in this time of a pseudo-intellectual evangelicalism, this is brushed aside with an impatient shrug of the shoulders, and they say, "Well, this is not so. The Bible is a skeptical scientific and philosophic proof." And so they are busy trying to prove the Word of God. God will pass over all these provers who rush in to prop up the Savior's throne with a matchstick. The Lord will let it all go, for the Lord whispers faith to the poor in spirit, to those who are child-like in heart, those who hate their sin and long after God, those who have heard the ancient whisper, and through the Word of the living God, they know, and they don't have to have any proof.

There was a wise man, St. Augustine, who said this in a rapturous outburst: "In Thee O God, lives the eternal reason of all things unreasoning and temporal."

Therefore, there are things temporal that are passing away. They come and go, and follow each other in their season, and man seeks for an anchor, somewhere to drive a spike into the universe and say, "This will never move from here, this is my anchor." There is one who longs for an absolute peg on which to hang all of his thoughts. He looks up to God and says, "O God, I believe in Thee are all the reasons," and he is ready to wait until that great day for the answer. God replies, "Wisdom is justified of all her children and all of the children of wisdom say amen, God. We do not understand, but we believe."

Therefore, a Christian is wise, not because he speaks with an Oxford accent, not because he understands half a dozen languages, although he may do both of those things, but he is wise for the thing that matters.

Even though the believing Christian asks no proof, he gets a lot of it. Even though he does not ask God to prove himself, God gives him a great witness, because, for one thing, the burden has lifted. Nobody can lift a burden except Jesus. The burden has lifted because he trusts the perfect wisdom of God in the cross and the atonement. I believe that when God created the heaven, the earth, and all things that are therein, He expressed wisdom, but not all His wisdom, because creation is limited and His wisdom is unlimited. I will say that everything He did in creation was done with a perfection of wisdom.

I believe that when He sent His holy Son to die, a portion of that creation went back to its Creator again, that creation being the human race. When He sent His Son to die on a cross, that could not have been improved upon if Abraham, David, Isaiah, Paul, Augustine, the archangels, and the seraphim had all pooled their knowledge. They could not have added to the perfection of the atonement because that was God dying on that cross, the only wise God our Savior. Therefore, when you say, "I am a Christian," what you are actually saying is, "I've geared into absolute wisdom and I rest upon that which cannot be improved upon: the cross, the blood, the atonement, the mediatorship of Jesus Christ; His advocacy at the right hand of the Father cannot be improved upon." God himself could not have done any better. That was an absolute. That was perfect. That was infinite, meaning holy without limit. Instead of spending time trying to prove the Bible is true, I believe it. I think *because* I believe; I do not think *in order to* believe.

A Christian gets an inward witness, not a proof, but an inward witness that becomes the proof, and his fear diminishes. Perfect love casts out fear, and I suppose if our love were perfect, there would be no fear whatsoever. If you are a true Christian, you do not have a third of the trouble you used to have. You are not worried a tenth as much as you used to be. While you cannot say honestly before God that you do not have certain haunting fears sometimes, your fears have diminished greatly, they are getting smaller and fewer as the years go by. To my mind, that is a witness of the wisdom of the Christian, and there has been a great change in his life.

Remember when you rarely read the Bible, but now you have one that is worn out? There have been some changes in your life all right, but we do not ask God, "O God, change me and I'll believe," we say, "God, I believe regardless, I believe no matter what."

We can identify with John Bunyan, "O God, I stand on the text and I'll go to hell standing on it." No man ever went to hell standing on the truth; he was simply willing to. It was the same with Moses, when he said, "O God, either forgive them or blot me out." God never blotted a righteous man out of His book, but Moses was willing for the sake of others, and that is all God wanted to know.

A Christian is happier than he used to be. I say some are not as happy as they should be. Our smiles are tentative and often our testimonies are as well. We say, "Pray for me. I thank the Lord I'm saved." It is good, but I think we ought to be happier, more confident. But we are happier than we used to be, and we are happier than the many who are not Christians. God puts joy into our souls, and our anxieties and worries begin to pass away.

Wisdom is justified of all her children. We appeal to you to become a Christian. We do not hold Jesus Christ up and say, "Won't you please believe on Him?" He is weeping for you. He wept blood once, but He is at the right hand of God the Father Almighty now, and on those great shoulders will someday rest the kingdoms of this world. When you are converted, you add nothing to His glory. If you refuse to be converted, you take nothing away from it. If you have heard the voice of God whisper in your heart, the wisest thing you can ever do for your own soul's sake is to come to God through Jesus Christ. Dare to believe that God is wise, that the call of God is wise, that the cross of Christ is wise, the blood of the lamb is wise, and God's redemptive plan is wise. When God sent His Son to die and worked out that marvelous, amazing, and wonderful way whereby He forgives you and me, He did it in utter wisdom.

It is a wise thing to be a Christian. It is extremely foolish to let yourself be caught up in the whirlpool of civilization, sucked down into the vortex of this world. You think it is wise? It is not wise, it is foolishness compounded. How wise the man who believes in Jesus Christ the Lord. He may have been a complete moral fool up to that time, but when he heard the voice of the invitation and accepted it, and believed in the only God who is perfectly wise and cast himself upon Jesus Christ and trusted Him, and continues to trust Him, that is the wisest thing he ever did.

Wisdom is justified of her children. If you stand up with any of the three major faiths, at your cathedral, your church, or your synagogue, nobody gets mad, no one is offended, but many are skeptical of those pesky traditionalists, those fundamentalists who believe in the blood of the Lamb, the new birth, and His coming again. They do not like us, we bother them, but there will be a day when it will be seen that we were wise because we embraced the absolute infinite perfect wisdom of God and His redemption.

☙ AWAKE, MY TONGUE, THY TRIBUTE BRING ❧

> But in redemption, O what grace!
> Its wonders, O what thought can trace!
> Here, wisdom shines forever bright;
> Praise Him, my soul, with sweet delight.
>
> John Needham

A Closing Prayer

Blessed Lord Jesus, ruler of all nature, O Thou of God and man, the Son, how we love Thee, how we praise Thee, how we bless Thee. In our folly, shame, and infamy we sought eagerly to satisfy ourselves; when it was done, it was not satisfying and left a hollow there, and we found nothing in it but emptiness. We thank Thee that we heard the voice of Jesus say, "Come unto me and rest." We came and laid our head upon the breast and heard the voice of Jesus say, "I am this dark world's light. Come unto me and thy morn shall rise and all the day be bright." I came to Thee and found in Thee my star, my sun, and the light of life. I will walk until my traveling days are done. O Jesus, Thou art so much that we do not even know how to pray. We stand before what Thou art as a little boy before a mountain, vast, illimitable, and awesome. Thou art all that we need and Thou art calling us to Thyself. Please do not allow us to lay our head on a pillow until we have turned from the folly of the fool to the wisdom of the just and sought to become another man indeed and be born again by faith in the shed blood and the atonement that Thou, O Christ, hast made for us.

O God, through Jesus Christ our Lord, we thank Thee for Thy suffering humanity. We cannot rise, Lord. We are born of earth and clay; we have bones and we cannot rise. We are hunkered down to earth by gravitational pull and we cannot rise and soar off. But O Lord Jesus, we can crawl into Thy suffering humanity, hide ourselves where the blood runs and find cleansing. Then Thou wilt lead us onward and upward through Thy blood, Lord Jesus, my righteousness, my glorious heavenly dress. In this inflaming world with joy shall I lift up my head, O Lord Jesus.

We praise Thee that we are not under the law, but under grace, and we walk no longer in the flesh, but in the Spirit. We praise Thee that thou wilt help us to learn the lesson and repent and continue repenting and putting all things under Thy feet. The lion and the dragon trampling every bad habit under their feet and putting behind them every wickedness until they are clean as clean can be, until the blood of Christ has made them holy.

Blessed Lord Jesus, we thank Thee that there is a voice heard wherever the Word is preached. It is heard in the conscience. Please let it continue to sound. We have not deserved it, Lord. If Thou were to suddenly take away from the world all the gospel calls and all the preachers and evangelists and missionaries, those who are working through your wisdom to say, "Come, come, come, why will you die?" If Thou were to remove them, Lord, we would have to stand and say, "True and righteous are Thy judgments." We deserved it, great God, but in Thy great mercy, Thou hast not yet removed them, and there is still hope for us all.

O Father, we pray Thou would strip away from us that veil hiding the future and make us wise to choose the wisdom of the just. Save us, we pray Thee, from being so weak we cannot say no to a suggestion. Save us from being so flabby that we cannot resist the urge to imitate somebody else. Great God, we would rather walk on our feet than to ride in the highest, greatest vehicle if to acquire it cost us our honesty. Great God, we would rather dwell in a tar-papered hut by the side of the railroad than to live on the Gold Coast if to live there cost us our righteousness and true holiness.

Father, we heard Thy Son say, "Thine they were, and Thou gavest them to me and I give unto them eternal life, and they shall never perish," and we hear Thy son say, "They shall all be taught of God and they that hear and are taught of the Father, they shall come to me and whoever comes to me I will in no wise cast out." Wilt Thou, we beseech Thee, continue to work deep within our hearts. Satan has every trap baited, every deadfall, every pit ready to catch unwary sinners, but Lord Jesus, Thou didst come to seek and to save that which was lost, and we pray that these might know in Thee saving grace and knowledge. Keep Thy hand upon us, we pray, and if it pleases Thee that these should believe and enter into a place of quiet and complete trust in a perfect Savior, grant that it may be so. In Jesus' name, amen.

A.W. Tozer (1897–1963) was a self-taught theologian, pastor, and writer whose powerful words continue to grip the intellect and stir the soul of today's believer. He authored more than forty books. *The Pursuit of God* and *The Knowledge of the Holy* are considered modern devotional classics. Get Tozer information and quotes at www.twitter.com/TozerAW.

Reverend James L. Snyder is an award-winning author whose writings have appeared in more than eighty periodicals and fifteen books. He is recognized as an authority on the life and ministry of A.W. Tozer. His first book, *The Life of A.W. Tozer: In Pursuit of God*, won the Reader's Choice Award in 1992 by *Christianity Today*. Because of his thorough knowledge of Tozer, James was given the rights from the A.W. Tozer estate to produce new books derived from over 400 never-before-published audiotapes. James and his wife live in Ocala, Florida. Learn more at www.jamessnyder.com.